"Turner crafts an amusing field guide to fundamentalism that's both a gentle lampoon of hypocrisy and misplaced fervor and a model of how to survive being 'churched' without cynically rejecting the good with the bad, the Founder with his followers."

—ANNA BROADWAY, author of *Sexless in the City*

"Matthew Paul Turner's memoir has the insight of Anne Lamott and the comic honesty of David Sedaris. His stories force us to wonder which of our Christian beliefs and practices come from Scripture and which spring up out of our own preferences and fears."

—ROB STENNETT, author of *The Almost True Story of Ryan Fisher*

"Finally! A bona fide humorist in the North American church! I might be tempted to say Matthew Paul Turner is Christendom's answer to David Sedaris, but Matthew stands on his own without the comparison. A memoirist who doesn't take himself or the world too seriously but still manages to write profoundly and beautifully, Turner gave me a belly laugh on almost every page. If you grew up believing 'being conformed not to this world' meant being the weirdest kid on the block, *Churched* will be the funniest book you've read in years!"

—LISA SAMSON, award-winning author of *Quaker Summer, Embrace Me,* and *Justice in the Burbs*

"With his homespun humor and eye for living detail, Matthew Paul Turner's *Churched* invites readers to rethink the quirks of Christian culture for the sake of uncovering that which is lastingly good and worth holding dear. Turner's work is a refreshingly gentle discussion of faith and culture that has the potential to spark meaningful conversations."

—PETE GALL, author of *My Beautiful Idol*

"If you didn't think Jesus-loving fundamentalist kids were very funny, Matthew Paul Turner proves you wrong."

—JASON BOYETT, author of *Pocket Guide to the Bible* and *Pocket Guide to the Apocalypse*

"How can a book be so stinkin' funny and yet so poignant at the same time? Matthew Paul Turner found his voice! After reading *Churched,* I wanted to hug him and then toss out all of my son's clip-on ties."

—JENNIFER SCHUCHMANN, author of *Six Prayers God Always Answers*

"Who knew that a journey through faith and fundamentalism could be so painfully funny? I laughed out loud many a time while reading *Churched.* Matthew Paul Turner manages to channel both boyhood innocence and wry retrospective through this fast-moving account of growing up with Jesus in late twentieth-century America and beyond."

—MIKE MORRELL, TheOoze.com

"A funny and heartfelt portrayal of one man's attempt to find true meaning despite his upbringing among fundamentalists who taught him that Azrael—the cat from *The Smurfs*—was an agent of Satan. The true miracle of this book is that its author never manages to lose his faith."

—ROBERT LANHAM, author of *Sinner's Guide to the Evangelical Right* churched

churched

one kid's journey toward God despite a holy mess

matthew paul turner

WATERBROOK
PRESS

CHURCHED
PUBLISHED BY WATERBROOK PRESS
12265 Oracle Boulevard, Suite 200
Colorado Springs, Colorado 80921
A division of Random House Inc.

Scripture quotations are taken from the King James Version.

The names of people have been changed as well as their identifying characteristics. In a couple of instances, composite characters have been created. For the sake of narrative flow, time lines have been condensed or modified.

ISBN 978-1-4000-7471-6

Copyright © 2008 by Matthew Paul Turner

Published in the United States by WaterBrook Multnomah, an imprint of The Doubleday Publishing Group, a division of Random House Inc., New York.

WATERBROOK and its deer colophon are registered trademarks of Random House Inc.

Library of Congress Cataloging-in-Publication Data
Turner, Matthew Paul, 1973–
    Churched : one kid's journey toward God despite a holy mess / Matthew Paul Turner. — 1st ed.
        p. cm.
    ISBN 978-1-4000-7471-6
    1. Turner, Matthew Paul, 1973– 2. Fundamentalism—United States. 3. Christian biography—United States. I. Title.
    BR1725.T785A3 2008
    277.3'082092—dc22
    [B]

                                    2008023783

Printed in the United States of America
2008—First Edition

10 9 8 7 6 5 4 3 2 1

SPECIAL SALES
Most WaterBrook Multnomah books are available in special quantity discounts when purchased in bulk by corporations, organizations, and special interest groups. Custom imprinting or excerpting can also be done to fit special needs. For information, please e-mail SpecialMarkets@WaterBrookMultnomah.com or call 1-800-603-7051.

For Elias

. . .

In thoughtful memory of Michael, Craig, and Rich

Contents

The riddles of God are more satisfying
than the solutions of man.

—G. K. CHESTERTON

Prelude

The man's shoulder was inked with a tattoo of Jesus breathing fire out of his mouth, which I concluded to mean one of two things: the man was going to offer me the opportunity to be born again in the hot fumes of a fire-breathing Messiah or he planned to kill me and make it necessary for me to *be* born again.

Like any "good" American, I had already been born again—since childhood I'd pretty much been on shuffle and repeat—but I still feared either scenario. I couldn't stop looking at the man's shoulder. His Jesus was green and faded, and because of a small mole, it appeared as though my Lord and Savior had a foreign object dangling from one nostril. Then the man looked at me from the opposite end of the sauna, tightened the towel around his waist, and said, "How are you, man? My name is Jim."

I didn't say anything at first. His question sort of paralyzed me. Would he pull a small Gideons Bible from somewhere underneath that towel, look up a bunch of frightful verses in Romans, and then ask me to get down on my hands and knees and repeat after him? I wouldn't do it. Not in a sauna. Not just wearing a towel. Besides, I had sworn off being born again *again* in this decade.

"Hello." I spoke carefully, still not ready to trust a person who had a flaming-tongue Messiah on an appendage. "My name is Matthew."

"Good to meet you, Matthew. Man, I don't know about you, but I have had the craziest day." Jim stared at me as he talked. I think he was making sure I paid attention. "I didn't even work out today. I just came right to the sauna." He stretched his arms and then massaged his left shoulder, pinching Jesus's face with his fingers.

I live in Nashville. The stereotypes about this town are true. Everyone is or has been a musician at some point in their life. Most of us who live here will carry on long conversations with people we don't know. When it rains here, the majority of us forget how to drive and become fully capable of killing ourselves. And everyone here has asked Jesus into their hearts at least once, if only to fulfill the requirements for getting a Tennessee driver's license.

But if I was going to stay true to the Nashville way, I would have to ask Jim to explain his "crazy day." That's not considered nosey in this town. He fully expected me to ask.

"What's been so crazy about your day?"

"Oh, just work, man. One of those days when you wonder whether or not you should have gotten out of bed."

"What kind of work do you do?"

"I'm an associate pastor at the Pentecostal church just up the road."

"The apostolic one?"

"Oh, you know it?"

"It's sort of difficult to miss."

"Yeah, I guess you're right. And it's about to get bigger. The deacon board just approved a ten-million-dollar expansion. Some of the members think we need a new *connection center.* I think it's a waste of money, but what are you going to do? So Matthew, are you a Christian?"

"I love *Jesus.* Does that count?"

Jim laughed as though he understood what I meant.

At the time, I was going through a period when I didn't like telling people I was a Christian. I didn't want them to be scared of me, fearing that I would invite them to church or a "rock concert" starring Kutless. And I didn't want them blaming me for the war in Iraq. Simply telling people I loved Jesus seemed like a cop-out to some of my friends, but often it kept me from having to own the sins of evangelicals in places like Kansas or South Carolina or two miles up the road at Jim's Pentecostal church.

"You know, man," said Jim, "I moved here a couple of years ago from Connecticut, where it's—*in my opinion*—spiritually dry. I thought moving here would make being a Christian a whole lot easier."

"Easier? Why did you think that?"

"Because Nashville is the Christian Mecca." Jim made air

quotes with his fingers when he said, "Christian Mecca." I'm sure he did it so I wouldn't assume he believed Nashville was Mecca or that Mecca was Christian.

Among Christians, air quotes are a form of contextualization. I'm partial to using them myself, mostly because they prevent somebody from taking a potentially rash or exaggerated statement and using it against me. "Wait just a minute," I can say to my antagonist. "I totally threw air quotes around the words *big fat loser* when describing the pastor. That clears me, man. I'm clean."

While they're not biblical, air quotes seem to sanctify insults and debatable theology like baptismal water sanctifies a baby's forehead.

But I understood Jim's point. While I'm quite sure religious people in places like Chicago and Detroit don't kneel southward when they say prayers to Jesus, I have met a good number of vacationers who come to Nashville because this city is a big ol' John Deere buckle in the Bible Belt.

"Seriously, think about it, Matthew. Do you know of any other city in America better known for its fear of God?" Jim wiped sweat off his brow. "I don't think I do."

I thought for a second. "I hear Colorado Springs is rather fearful."

"I'm sure that's true. But I doubt it's Nashville. I've been told this town has more churches per capita than any other city in America." Jim nodded. "Honest-to-God truth, Matthew, that's what I've been told by a number of people, and I can believe it."

I believed it too. No doubt we have a lot of churches in this town. But since I've heard the same statistic used in reference to Dallas, Birmingham, and Orlando, I'm not sure it's scientific. But scientific matters don't hold much weight in Christian cultural claims, so it probably wouldn't count even if proven.

Even if Nashville doesn't lead with the *most* churches, I've always said that one of this city's chief exports is Jesus. God's only Son gets shipped, bused, couriered, radioed, televised, faxed, e-mailed, and, if need be, dropped like a bomb from twenty thousand feet in places all over the world because of what happens here in Nashville. In many ways, we are God's command center. His Pentagon. His newer Jerusalem.

With a push of a button, we can have a million Bibles dropped in a remote location in China. With a phone call or two, we can get a person carrying some very good news to show up on your doorstep, like Publishers Clearing House. The only catch is, you have to die before you're able to afford that mansion you've always dreamed of.

Jim and I walked out of the sauna to cool off. He sat on one of the benches, and I went over to the water fountain.

"So tell me why you thought moving to Nashville would make it easier to be a Christian," I said.

He laughed. "Because Christians are everywhere. I thought it would be amazing to be in a city where Jesus is as much a part of the culture as Dolly and Cracker Barrel."

I laughed. "Okay, I get that. I've probably been there at some point in my life."

"I also thought it would make being a pastor a lot easier.

I mean, back home I would never have had this kind of conversation with somebody at the gym. Here, it happens every time I work out. It's almost annoying. Sometimes it feels like we're playing church. It's difficult to explain."

"But I understand what you're saying."

I'd been looking for a way to ask about the tattoo, but with no open window, I just blurted, "Jim, you have to tell me the deal with the tattoo."

"You mean you don't like it?" He laughed. "Man, I was young. I guess it was my way of sharing the truth about Jesus without having to say anything."

"And that truth would be what? That Jesus is a flame-thrower? Puff, the Magic Dragon?"

"Dude, I was an idiot back then. Now, I'm embarrassed to go to a public pool where people who don't know me can see me without a shirt. I'm scared to death somebody will take it seriously."

"I kind of did. It's one of the most awful tattoos I've ever seen. I'd call that 'doctor'—you know, the one who advertises on 107.5—and have that thing removed."

I headed back to the sauna for another round. For a few minutes, I sat there alone, thinking about my conversation with Jim.

I wasn't a pastor, but I had been to church more times than I could count, and I had lived in Nashville for a while, so I knew something about what he felt. At first, this town feels like a shot of faith in the arm.

When I first moved here, I thought it was energizing to be a part of a community where you were odd if you didn't believe in Jesus. I felt at home. Even alive at times. But I started thinking about it too much, which led me to wonder if I was just filling a role in a *Stepford*-type reality.

Jim opened the sauna door, stepped inside, and sat down. He didn't say anything, so I didn't either.

My mind wandered back to a service I attended at one of Nashville's largest churches a year or so after moving here. I hadn't really wanted to go, but a friend begged me. "It's our annual Harvest Festival on Sunday," he told me. "You'll love it. Please come. God always shows up on Harvest Sunday."

Against my better judgment, I agreed to go with him. I didn't want to miss an event that God had in his Day-Timer. Taking our seats in the balcony, my friend said, "They're expecting something like fifteen thousand people. An extra service had to be added. Just think about how many people will be saved today." He shook his head like people do at the circus while watching the trapeze act or when Spider-Man shows up to save the day. My friend was anticipating acrobats and special effects.

By the time the choir filled the loft, the room was packed, and the orchestra began playing an old hymn. I knew the song from the first notes.

"Bringing in the Sheaves." I used to sing it when I was a kid. Back then, I knew every word, but I didn't understand what they meant until much later.

The choir began singing the first verse.

Sowing in the morning,
Sowing seeds of kindness…

Hearing that old song reminded me of the time my father and I went to a neighbor's farm and picked a bushel of sweet corn right off the stalks. The farmer had a lengthy driveway. As we drove over the bumpy gravel, Dad pointed out a golden wheat field.

"That wheat is ready to harvest, Buck." My father's eyes brightened any time he saw a ripened field of wheat, corn, or anything edible. "You know, when I was a kid, harvest was one of my favorite times of the year. Workers came from all over the county and helped us bundle up the wheat into sheaves. It was such an important day for us, sort of our payday. I remember Daddy being so particular about his crop, making sure those workers got every piece of wheat in that field. He'd get so mad when somebody wasn't doing a good job; he'd go behind the workers and pick up whatever they left."

My friend's pastor only mentioned the word *harvest* once during his sermon. He didn't talk about wheat fields and never mentioned a sheave. He asked, "Have you given any thought to what will happen on Judgment Day?"

Then he directed the sermon toward the members of his church. "Church, souls are being lost every single day. *Why?* Because we aren't doing our job. We aren't out harvesting

God's crop. People are going to get left behind because of you and me."

I sank back into my pew, my heart feeling anxious. I'd heard that same message a million times, it seemed, but rather than making me feel hopeful, on that day the Good News scared me. I thought about my grandfather. Even he didn't want to leave any wheat in the field.

I could only imagine God feeling the same way.

Jim jarred me out of my thoughts. "You think this is what hell feels like?"

"You talking about the sauna or living in Nashville?"

He smiled. "The sauna."

"Then I doubt it. I like this too much."

"Well, I guess I'd better get going. I have a meeting with my pastor tonight. He's convinced that I don't speak in tongues."

"And that's a problem?"

"Of course—we're Pentecostals. It's what we do."

"Sounds like your church might have a little baggage." My grin faded. "But who am I to judge? I'm still unpacking my own."

God's New Digs

It happened when I was almost five. I got yanked out of my life as an ordinary kid and plopped into a small fundamentalist church. The experience was kind of like being kidnapped by Puritans, except without a witch trial and a dunking booth. An easygoing kid with undiagnosed ADHD, I was bright-eyed, charismatic, and inquisitive. Looking back, I'm inclined to think I would have made a really good beagle.

On my first Sunday morning as an independent fundamental Baptist, my mother walked into my bedroom and scoured my closet in hopes of finding me something uncomfortable to wear.

"You're dressing up for church this morning, Matthew." Mom pulled out a pair of pants and some black socks and then looked at me like she was thoughtfully considering eating me for breakfast. "Which *means* you're wearing a tie."

She tossed my navy blue clip-on across my lap.

"Please don't argue with me this morning. If you do, I'm getting your father involved and letting him deal with it."

Mom turned her back toward me and rummaged through my closet for my black belt.

"I really mean it, Matthew. I don't feel like arguing with you this morning. I have a lot on my mind."

Thinking too much made my mother's complexion pasty, like somebody with the stomach flu or a sun allergy. Whenever Mom looked pale, she was usually preoccupied with something. And on that morning her face looked as white as a bowl full of Cream of Wheat.

I had the same problem but without the telltale pallor. Sometimes my four-year-old brain felt as overworked as a somersaulting circus dog.

That Sunday, the new church weighed on Mom's mind. She and Dad had come to the conclusion that God wasn't attending our old church and it didn't make sense to go to a place even God didn't want to go to.

One afternoon a young pastor named Dave Nolan knocked on our door. He talked to my parents for more than an hour. I only heard bits and pieces of the story, but the gist of their conversation was about a brand-new church he was starting. Mom and Dad seemed to think Pastor Nolan's visit was a message from God.

I've learned over the years that getting messages from God is a lot like getting a brand-new package of Silly Putty. On that first day it seems like the greatest gift in the world. It's all you can think about. You play with it nonstop. But the more you squash it around in your hands, press it up against stuff to see if it sticks, and allow other people to put their mucky hands all over it, the dirtier and less impressive it becomes. Within three days, you're bored with it, the protective shell it came in is cracked, and you think it might be growing some hair. I was pretty certain Mom had thought and rethought our church move into a nasty little blob of dirt-and-fuzz-covered putty hiding underneath the couch.

"Do you want to wear your white dress shirt or your blue dress shirt?" Mom held both selections so I could see them. I pointed to the white one. "Okay, now for shoes."

As my mother hunted down my black church shoes, I sat on the edge of my bed and bounced like the fiberglass Scooby-Doo ride at the A&P. Mom searched but kept an eye on me. I think she was waiting for me to complain about the tie. Not that day. I was far too excited about the new church to complain.

Under ordinary circumstances, the mere thought of wearing a necktie caused me to fall onto the floor in hysterics. I'd wail like a siren, beat my hands against the carpet, and kick my feet against anything they could reach. To this day, I believe I had an excellent reason for having a seizure whenever the idea of wearing a clip-on necktie was posed, but my mother thought I was being ridiculous. She found it difficult to believe that every one of my clip-on ties licked my neck when she wasn't looking.

"It *really* happens, Mom," I explained to her once.

"Then why haven't I seen it happen?"

"I guess you aren't looking at the right times."

"Is that so?"

"Yes. As soon as you turn your head, the tie sticks its tongue out at you and then starts licking me."

"Oh, so the tie does that? That's impossible, Matthew."

Sometimes talking to my mother felt like explaining Jesus to my Uncle Ramil, who was from Uzbekistan. She would look at me with her eyebrows raised and patronizingly nod her head as if she completely understood everything I was talking about, when, in truth, she didn't even speak my language.

"What's wrong with Matthew, hon?" My father's question gave me hope.

"Oh, he says his clip-on tie is, and I quote, '*licking* his neck.'"

My father laughed. "You think he's imagining it?"

"I bought them at Sears, Virgil. You'd think it would be on the news or something if Sears was selling perverted neckties. Am I right?"

I should have known my father would take my mother's side. He wore the kind of neckties that wrapped around your neck and choked you from the front, not the kind with tongues that hung on to your shirt for dear life.

"You are going to look so handsome this morning, young man." My mother helped me shove my head through my T-shirt and then helped me put on my dress shirt.

"Mom." I watched her fingers start at the bottom of my shirt and button their way to the top. "Do you really think God will be at our new church?"

"I think God is always with us."

"You do?"

Mom nodded her head.

"Do you think I'll see him this morning?"

"I guess we'll have to wait and see, now, won't we?" Mom tucked my shirt in with one hand and held on to my pants with the other so they wouldn't fall down. "What I do know is—you might not like wearing it, but this tie is going to perfectly match these new plaid pants I bought you."

Mom snapped the front button of my pants, smoothed out the wrinkles on my shirt with her hands, and then picked up my navy blue necktie and clipped it to the top button of my shirt.

As soon as she buttoned down my collar, the clip got fresh with my clavicle.

"There, that's perfect." Mom patted my shoulder and gave me a peck on the cheek. "Now, that's not so bad, is it?"

It wasn't bad at all. In fact, I was starting to enjoy getting kissed by polyester.

"Look at you." The color in Mom's face seemed to be coming back. "I think you look like the perfect little Baptist, if I say so myself."

Mom walked out of my bedroom and left me standing in front of my mirror. *A perfect little Baptist?* I thought. I didn't see that. As far as I was concerned, I looked exactly the same as I had the Sunday before, except I was wearing a pair of pants that matched the dining-room tablecloth.

I felt uncool, but definitely not Baptist.

Going to church was not a new thing for me. Mom and Dad rolled me into my first church service and parked my stroller next to their pew when I was eight weeks old. I've been told that all the important people at my church walked up to me that day and put their faces in my stroller, spoke to me in strange tongues, and poked my belly. I didn't get much out of that first worship service. All I did was sleep, pass gas, and wet my diaper. But a large portion of that congregation was older than the cotton gin, so I wasn't much of a novelty.

Before we switched churches, my mother and father weren't Christians. They were Methodists. That's what they wrote down when the last census had come around. I suppose, to my parents, merely jotting down "Christian" only differentiated them from Jews, Muslims, or Buddhists, which wasn't good enough.

"Who in the world is going to think we're Buddhists?" My father had a very practical, albeit *frank*, way of looking at things. "We're white people from Maryland. We hunt things. I bet there's not one Buddhist within fifty miles of here. I'd be much more concerned about someone thinking we're Catholic."

I grew up in Kent County, Maryland, where most people who were Methodists had been born that way. That was true for my mother. Her religion was hereditary. Mom inherited her *Methodistness* from her mother's side of the family, but my father hadn't been born with any identifiable religious gene. His faith was sort of bestowed upon him at the age of nine when his mother started feeling guilty about her family not being religious.

My grandmother set out to change that by making an appointment with the local minister of the Methodist church. Sitting in his office, she told the preacher all about the predicament she was in. He thought he might be able to help. A few days later, she invited the minister over for dinner. After he finished his meal, the minister pushed away from the table and began putting on a water-resistant poncho.

"I wear this so I don't get my suit splashed. You'd be surprised how wet one can get while baptizing."

He then told my grandmother to arrange her six children—two boys and four girls—in a line from oldest to youngest. The minister stood in the kitchen and, after he recited the Lord's Prayer, splashed each kid's face with tap water in the name of the Father, the Son, and the Holy Spirit.

"Well, Ruth, it's official. Your kids are now full-fledged Methodists." The preacher grinned at the children as if he'd just finished giving each of them a shot in the backside, which my father seems to think was appropriate. He says his mother wasn't so much trying to introduce her children to Jesus as she was sort of vaccinating them in the hope they wouldn't become cult members, alcoholics, or—*God forbid*—Episcopalians. "If you need anything at all, Ruth, you know where to find me."

At the time, my family belonged to St. James United Methodist Church, just two miles from our home. The congregation met in an old building built in the early nineteen hundreds. In its heyday, St. James boasted a large attendance, but those days were long gone. Though the church had 350 members on record, many were people who had either moved or were buried in the church's backyard. By the time I was old enough to remember St. James, there were about 60 of us attending on Sunday mornings. My parents were active members. In addition to being on the church's board of directors, my father also taught a boys' Sunday school class. My mother led the children's choir and coached the girls' youth-group basketball squad. It was ministry at its finest.

Our church was located in close proximity to the Chesapeake Bay, which was a big deal. During the summer months, when the boaters were in town for their weekends of fishing, crabbing, and debauchery, our church became a tourist attraction. The sinners didn't join us for Sunday service; they just drove by our church to gawk at our rather impressive steeple. For quite some time, St. James had been known for having one of the biggest steeples in the district. On Sundays after church, we'd usually see seven or eight cars with fancy hood ornaments drive by to marvel at our holy monstrosity.

"Gosh, rich people are so strange. Look at them stretching their heads out of their cars. They look like turkeys." Miss Edith was the oldest woman in our church. Each Sunday during the summer, she and a friend sat out on the church's front steps and watched tourists drive by. "Good Lord, Joyce, that car came all the way from New Jersey." She squinted her eyes as she looked. "I don't think you could pay me to live in New Jersey. All that smog. I don't know how people up there do it."

I watched her take a deep breath, pull out her driving glasses, and then light a cigarette. As she took her first drag, the expression on her face was glorious, as though she was slowly inhaling the Holy Spirit. "They act like they've never seen a church before. That's because they're from New Jersey."

"You should have been here last Sunday, Edith." Miss Joyce waved her hand in front of her face to chase away the cigarette smoke. "I bet you ten cars went by. George and I sat here for almost thirty minutes and watched car after car roll down its windows and gaze up at our steeple. One of the women even took a picture."

Miss Edith's mouth dropped open, and her eyes widened, making her look like a slot machine.

"They took a picture? Lord knows, if people are going to take photographs of our steeple, then somebody should get up there and paint the darn thing. If you ask me, it's starting to get a little crusty." Miss Edith looked both ways like she was getting ready to slide off the steps and across a street. "Like the preaching has been lately."

Miss Edith took a second look around and then nodded her head. "I mean, seriously, Joyce. *Yertle the Turtle?* What kind of preacher uses a Dr. Seuss book as the basis for his sermon?"

"You don't have to say another word, Edith. I know exactly what you mean. I told my George, 'How in the world is someone supposed to find God in a fairy tale about an amphibian?'"

"What'd he say?"

"He thought it was ridiculous. And, as you know, my George studied biology."

Pastor Dean Woody liked to believe one could find God in a variety of things. Unfortunately for him, a number of St. James's oldest members thought his theory was a bunch of hogwash. A couple of the parishioners even suggested that they didn't believe God would be found dead in some of the junk Pastor Woody mentioned during his sermons.

The Dr. Seuss fiasco resulted in my parents' wondering whether or not God was showing up for services at St. James.

On one Sunday morning, my father and I arrived at church early. While Dad set up his Sunday school classroom, I decided to see if I could find God. I had heard Pastor Woody say on a couple of occasions that if two were gathered together, God was there. Since Dad and I made two, I thought my chances of finding God were pretty good.

The first place I searched was the church sanctuary. I thought God might prefer being around crosses, the altar, and the walnut floors. But when I searched under the pews, inside the pulpit, around the choir loft, underneath the piano, and in the storage closet, I didn't see God. After that, I looked inside each of the Sunday school classrooms. Then I opened and closed all of the cupboards and drawers in the kitchen. I even checked the men's room. God seemed to be missing.

"Why can't I find God?" I asked my Sunday school teacher, Miss Thelma, who was, in my opinion, the manliest woman I had ever seen. On top of that, Miss Thelma lived on a dairy farm, so she came to Sunday school smelling like she had rolled around on the ground with the cows. But I loved Miss Thelma. In fact, if I held my nose, I was able to believe she knew more about God than anyone else in the world.

"I tried looking for God this morning," I said to her, "and I couldn't find him anywhere."

Miss Thelma smiled big, stood up from the table, and walked toward me.

Since she was looking right at me, it would have been impolite for me to hold my nose. I took a deep breath and held it, and I tried really hard to pretend I wasn't holding my breath.

"Matthew, here's the thing." Miss Thelma kneeled next to my chair and tapped her hand against my arm.

"Seeing God takes more than simply looking for him with your eyes or listening for him with your ears. It takes faith, Matthew. And faith isn't something we often experience with our five senses."

Unlike cow manure, I thought, letting the air slowly seep out of my lungs.

"Have you seen God?" I asked, then took another breath and held it.

"Yes, I think so, Matthew. I think I see him every Sunday in the faces and grins of you kids." She looked around the room. Miss Thelma put her arm around me and gave me a sideways hug. She stood up, and as she walked away, I exhaled.

After catching my breath, I looked around the room at all the other kids and tried to find God in the faces of my classmates. But since they were eating animal crackers and drinking fruit punch, all I saw were crumb-covered mouths and lips that had been artificially turned red by Hawaiian fruit punch. My mother was convinced that anything containing artificial food coloring was godless. She wasn't a fan of crumbs either, so if God was there, he was up to no good.

Sunday mornings, I knew when it was time to leave for church. Whenever the house was overtaken by the scent of my father's cologne, I had better find my Bible and be prepared to walk out the back door. Dad wasn't a sophisticated man when it came to his personal scent. The musky sweet aroma he wore on Sunday mornings cost him nine dollars at Drug Fair and made him smell like he'd been stir-fried in a wok. But it served a purpose. Every member of the family knew it was time to leave for church as soon as the house started smelling like Kung Pao chicken.

That was a sure sign that within a couple of minutes Dad

would make his Sunday morning pilgrimage from the bedroom to the garage. We'd hear him walk down the hallway, shutting off lights, closing bedroom doors, and complaining under his breath about the price of electricity.

My father's easy stride never broke rhythm during the week, a walk reminiscent of a farmer trekking across a cornfield. That was how he walked on Mondays at work or on Friday afternoons hunting hedgerows for rabbits.

But on Sunday mornings he walked differently. Less casual. He leaned his body forward a little more and looked up and around a lot less. Sometimes, usually when it was very humid outside, he favored his right leg. His was an intentional swagger, the kind that told me he believed in where he was going and I should too.

"Carole," my father yelled from the kitchen. "Let's go, hon! It's almost 8:35. I don't want to be late on our first Sunday."

By the time my mother was ready to walk out the door, the rest of us had crammed into our blue Chevy Caprice, and Melanie and Kelley were begging my father to not honk the horn for Mom. As she stepped into the car, Dad's eyes looked like eightballs.

"I don't want to hear one word out of you, Virgil." My mother was pale again, and she fanned herself with both hands. "You *had to have pancakes.* And *scrapple.* All of that takes time. It's not my fault if we're late."

Mom turned the passenger vent toward her face. "Is it hot in here? I'm burning up."

"I'm not hot," Dad said. My sisters shook their heads.

"You're really not hot?" Mom leaned back against the seat and stared out the window. "Virgil, we're sure about this, right? You know, about switching churches and all?"

My father laughed. "This started out as your idea."

"I know. But we're sure it's a good one, right?"

"I've got no qualms about it, hon." Dad smiled and gently squeezed my mother's thigh.

That was all my mother needed—to know that Dad was sure.

As I got older, I learned that Dad's certainty in a decision simply meant that what he had decided was inevitable—like taxes or death or a moral lesson at the end of *Little House on the Prairie*. Being sure didn't always mean it was a good decision. It just meant that, whether he liked it or not, he would have to learn to live with it. And the rest of us would too.

A few minutes later, Dad turned into a parking lot.

"Is this where God moved?" I pressed one side of my face up against the car's back window.

"Isn't this the Board of Education building?" asked Kelley. "I think I've been here before."

"Probably where you took summer school last year," said Melanie.

"Shut up. This wasn't where I took summer school."

"Where's the steeple, Dad?" I asked. "There's no steeple. How can we have church without a steeple?"

"Mom," said Melanie, "isn't this where your friend Pearl works?"

Mom nodded.

"Dad." I pulled at the hem of my father's suit jacket. "How is God going to know where to show up without a steeple?"

"God will find us, Buck. Trust me, he'll find us."

The Fundamentals

On my sixth Sunday as a Baptist, I wasn't in a huge hurry, so rather than running, I decided to take my time and trot like a pony through the front doors of the Board of Education building. I would have preferred to skip into church, but my father didn't like his only son frolicking around like a schoolgirl. He once informed me that my skipping reminded him of a guy named Tiny Tim. I had never met Tiny, but Dad said he was a happy fellow who enjoyed singing and tiptoeing through tulips. Tiny didn't sound like a bad guy to me, but my father was adamant. "Men don't skip, Buck."

So I took up trotting instead. Trotting wasn't all that different from skipping, but because I could trot without flailing my arms, I suppose I looked less like Goldilocks.

Just as I passed through the entranceway, en route to the row of seats Melanie would be saving for our family, a very old, elflike man stopped me in my tracks.

"Now, where do you think you're going, young man?" Santa's helper bent at the waist, his face just six inches from mine. "How's Brother Matthew doing this morning?"

"Good," I said.

The large elf was Mr. Flamerson, a deacon at my church, who was nice but would not let me walk into church without throwing a couple of air punches at my gut. The first time was fun and I laughed. The second time was tolerable. By the third Sunday, I had to sneak in through one of the side doors to avoid what was obviously going to be a weekly boxing match.

"Okay, little man, be on your way," he said, giving me one more air punch to the shoulder and letting out a big belly laugh, one that sounded like it came from a faraway body part that I was pretty sure I hadn't developed yet.

Mr. Flamerson seemed to think I had nothing better to do than stand there and pretend I was really getting a beat-down by his sad little punches. But I *always* had something to do or someplace to go. That Sunday, I was on my way to borrow one of my sisters' Bibles so I could look up a Scripture verse my friend Willie had said contained a bad word.

"What kind of bad word?" I'd asked him.

"I'm not allowed to say it. Go look it up yourself."

"You're lying. There's no bad words in the Bible."

"I'm not lying. You can look it up."

When I found the verse in question, I took the Bible to my father and pointed at the word. I figured I shouldn't use it in case Willie had been onto something when he suggested that God said cusswords sometimes. "Dad, Willie says that word right *there*"—I placed my finger right next to the word in question—"is bad. Is it?" I looked up at my father's face.

"*Bad?* That word isn't bad. It means donkey, son. You go tell Willie that he doesn't know what he's talking about. God doesn't say bad words."

After church that day, as I told Willie that he didn't know what he was talking about, I happened to say out loud the word God preferred to use instead of donkey. As soon as I said it, I heard the distinct tone of my mother's voice ringing like a siren in my ear.

"Matthew Turner, what did I just hear you say?"

I turned around and repeated for my mother God's word for donkey.

"Matthew, that's a *bad* word."

"Dad told me it meant donkey."

Mom's tone dropped to a gentler decibel. "Well, it does mean donkey, but it's not a word to say at church."

"But, Mom, it's in the Bible. Willie found it."

"Yes, but it's talking about a *donkey* in the Bible."

"I was talking about a donkey too." I leaned closer and whispered. "Are donkeys bad?"

"No, son, donkeys aren't bad, but we call them donkeys and not the other word."

"But why is it okay for God to use it?"

My mother placed her Bible in front of her and put her knees on top of it so her nylons wouldn't touch the gravel. She was eye level with me as she explained that some words change over time. She said that because the Bible was written so long ago, a couple of the words it uses have new meanings now. "The Bible's word for donkey is one of those words."

"Really?" I said. "What does it mean now?"

"That's not important. Maybe when you're older, I'll tell you what it means, but for now, don't use it."

"Yes ma'am."

I had only been Baptist for a few weeks, but it was already clear that the God who came to the Baptist church was a lot more particular than the one I heard Methodists talk about— or he was schizophrenic. Of course, at the time, I hadn't taken any psych courses, so I concluded that the Baptist God just did things differently than the Methodist God. I recognized some of those differences on our first Sunday at Independent Baptist Bible Church. This new God we worshiped had much more charisma than the Methodist God, but he also seemed to enjoy interfering a lot more in my personal space. I wasn't sure what to think about him.

As soon as I found a seat on that first Sunday, I got down on all fours and stuck my nose against the tile floor like a hunting dog. It never occurred to me I was doing something odd.

"What on earth are you doing?" My sister Melanie barked at me as if she'd never once been tempted to smell linoleum.

Eleven years older than me, Melanie liked to think of herself as my second mother.

"I'm smelling the floor tiles." I didn't look up at her. I kept my nose to the ground and searched for a familiar scent.

"Why are you smelling the floor tiles?" she shrieked.

"I was hoping *this* church smelled like our old one."

"St. James had a scent?"

"Yes."

I thought St. James had a wonderful scent, like a freshly cleaned cage for gerbils or hamsters, a sweet aroma of cedar chips and processed alfalfa. None of the members of St. James were small, unnecessary mammals, but the building seemed to have the perfect odor for a house that God lived in.

"You're wasting your time," said Melanie, moving toward me and hanging over me like my own personal rain cloud.

"Why am I wasting my time?"

"First, our old church had hardwood floors, Matthew, and second, this floor is filthy." She reached down and pulled at my arm.

"Really? It doesn't smell filthy."

"Well, that doesn't matter. I think you should get up. You look ridiculous, like you don't have any sense. But more importantly, somebody might have peed on it or something."

I looked up at her.

"It's possible," she said, crossing her arms. "You want to get urine up your nostrils?"

Melanie's science teacher had just taught her class about

odors and how they were actually made up of millions of molecular particles. For that reason, she didn't like to take a deep breath of anything. She feared her nostrils would fill up with food, sweat, or household cleaning products.

I shook my head.

"But what if they make us kneel during the service?" I asked.

"They won't make us do that."

"How do you know?"

"Baptists don't kneel unless there's an altar call going on."

I stood up and brushed the dust off my knees. My oldest sibling knew a good deal about churchy matters, so trusting her wisdom was easy.

Melanie loved God more than any teenager I knew. Some people thought my sister acted a little uppity about it, like a nun who was proud of how she looked in baggy black-and-white garb, but my sister had a reason to be that way. She had been one of the most well-behaved teenagers at St. James and a preacher's pet. She knew what becoming a fundamentalist would do to her dating life, and yet that made it more appealing. Oftentimes, Melanie didn't seem very much like a teenager. More like a forty-year-old virgin who hadn't stopped shopping in the juniors' department at Strawbridge's.

The summer prior to my family becoming Baptist, Melanie went with the St. James youth group to a Christian festival. For three days, she camped on a Pennsylvania hillside with thousands of people who grew their hair out long, sat around campfires, and inhaled the Holy Spirit. When she returned home, Melanie no longer walked—she hovered. After two days, my sister Kelley got sick of Melanie floating around the house singing Jesus songs, so my father told her she was only allowed to play with the Holy Ghost on Sundays and Wednesday afternoons.

"You need to sit still." Melanie patted my chair. "You can't run around the auditorium at this church. We're not Methodist anymore."

I climbed onto a chair. I hadn't heard the first sermon yet and already our family showed signs of being uptight and boring. I looked around, taking in the view above floor level.

The Baptist men seemed to dress up more than the men at the Methodist church. All of them wore suits and ties, and some wore vests. A polo shirt and khakis weren't proper apparel for this house of God, it seemed.

"I don't think a man should walk into church looking like he's getting ready to play eighteen holes of golf," Pastor Nolan told my father on a later occasion. The men listened to him too—not one of them appeared to have arrived at church for fun and relaxation. Most of them looked like they were there to sell cars, talk about insurance, or carry a casket. One man did seem to be more comfortable than the others. His shirt had stripes of various widths and colors running vertically and horizontally across his chest.

My sister Kelley said it looked like a souvenir he probably purchased while on vacation in Texas or Nashville. The man didn't seem to care that it didn't match the tweed suit jacket he wore or that he clashed with all the other men. Rather than donning a standard tie, around his neck he'd tied a small black ribbon, something that might have made a fitting barrette in the hair of a child whose parents were in mourning or practicing vampires.

"That man used to be a *Mennonite,* Matthew. Isn't that neat?" My mother said the word *Mennonite* the same way she'd say Tweety Bird or Grover or Father Abraham, like it was supposed to thrill me. "That's why he's wearing that black ribbon around his neck."

One difference about IBBC stood above all others: the people were excited about God. Even though they dressed for a funeral, they smiled and laughed a lot more than the people at St. James. And smoked a lot less. Maybe their joy was simply the idealism of beginning something new. Or maybe nerves caused them to grin as though an Olan Mills photographer was coaxing them from behind a camera. But compared to the sarcastic smirks of those at the old church, the smiles of my new church family were a beautiful sight and filled my heart with excitement for the future.

As the chords from an upright piano filled the room, people scurried around the church, marking their territory with coats, pocketbooks, and Bibles.

The woman behind the piano was Laura Nolan, Pastor Nolan's wife. She was rumored to be a professional wife with a three-year degree in pastoral wifery. I only knew her as the

woman in our church who made walking in high heels a reason for even the holiest of Baptists to stop reading their Bibles
and stare. My first thought upon seeing her hips shift grace-
fully back and forth as she moved from her chair to the piano
bench was that she looked exactly like Farrah Fawcett.

As far as I was concerned, God had been far too kind to
Pastor Nolan. Mrs. Farrah was the most beautiful woman I
had ever seen in 3-D. Even if you weren't enamored with her
walk or her stunning appearance, you couldn't help but stare
at her fingers when they paraded across the piano keys like a
harem of angels marching to Zion—beautiful, beautiful
Zion. Mrs. Farrah's fingers bounced up and down on the key-
board, and her eyes never once glanced at the music. She
looked around the room as if she hardly noticed that her
hands were pounding out a booming version of "A Mighty
Fortress Is Our God."

The woman sitting behind me liked the song played that
bracing.

"I bet Martin Luther would have wanted it just like that."
Miss Grace tapped her hand against her knee to the beat of
the music.

I knew her name was Grace because she was the only person in the church who had brought her own name tag. It was
clipped to her pink sweater. "Hello, I'm Grace," it read. To
me, those words made her seem friendlier than everybody else
in the church. I thought everybody could have used a sign on
their shirt that announced their name. I would have wanted

mine to read, "Hey, I'm Matthew P. Turner. Since you're already staring at my chest, please feel free to say hello to me. I'm very nice."

Miss Grace had the whitest hair I'd ever seen. She seemed proud of its whiteness. She had obviously spent a lot of time in front of the mirror, poufing it perfectly in every direction as if she'd set out to look exactly like a Q-tip.

I wanted to touch it.

After Mrs. Farrah finished playing her hymn of mass destruction, a man named Jonesy stood up and read seven announcements. He was a distinguished-looking gentleman who, according to my father, had more money in his front shirt pocket than Dad would make all year long. After he finished making announcements about a church potluck and an upcoming Sunday school series called "How to Be a Fundamentalist," Jonesy smiled and said, "Isn't it good to be in God's house this morning?"

That seemed like a strange question, considering that in twenty-four hours God's house was scheduled to become a room where all the dumb kids from our county would take their summer school classes, but that didn't stop people from applauding and nodding their heads. Jonesy then introduced Pastor Nolan.

Pastor Nolan and Mrs. Laura had moved to Chestertown to start Independent Baptist Bible Church right after graduating from Fyles Sanderson College in Indiana. Nobody seemed to know exactly *how* Fyles Sanderson was able to manufacture Christians into professional holy-rolling Baptists, but someone once told me it was similar to how poultry plants turned whole chickens into fryable bite-sized nuggets. Whatever the process, it had worked, and Pastor Nolan and Mrs. Laura were quality Baptists, shining examples for us to follow and obey.

Pastor Nolan might have been a plain-looking fellow with beady eyes and a comb-over, but that was just his "disguise"— like Lynda Carter without a boomerang headband keeping her hair in place or when she wasn't saving the world in a stars-stripes-and-eagle swimsuit. Pastor Nolan didn't turn into Wonder Woman, but anytime he stood behind a pulpit, he did morph into "God Man"—not *Jesus,* but a hero whose motto was Defender of Truth, Judgment, and Morality for All. Some people called what happened to him when he stepped behind a pulpit "an anointing." That was a holy term people at my church used whenever a human seemed to be subleasing God's power and authority. Pastor Nolan rented the attributes of God every Sunday morning, Sunday evening, and Wednesday evening.

That first morning, his sermon was about Daniel, an eloquent, albeit loud, presentation about the prophet who slept overnight with lions and didn't get eaten. During the sermon, Pastor Nolan wandered onto a couple of bunny trails. This was normally when his messages from God became interesting. Speaking about Daniel gave him an opportunity to rail against people who worked for companies that made beer, and at one point he told us he believed there was somebody in our church living in a lion's den.

During Pastor Nolan's sermon, I realized something about him: God had created him without a noticeable neck. From my vantage point, it looked as though his bald head sat atop his shoulders like a bowling ball. Without proper balance on his part, his head might roll off onto the floor and create an awful mess.

I thought of the pictures I'd seen of African women who balanced bowls the size of small Volkswagens on their heads as they walked for miles. Then they picked up their kids from school, put a day's worth of food in the trunk, and walked home. I suppose Pastor Nolan was lucky to just have to worry about maintaining his head's equilibrium, not packing it like a station wagon.

A few weeks later, while riding home from church, I leaned forward and stuck my head on the front seat between my father and mother. "I have a question."

My mother looked at me with raised eyebrows, signaling interest.

"Does Pastor Nolan have a neck?" I looked at Mom, then Dad.

"Does Pastor Nolan have a neck?"

I got the impression my mother didn't think my question was appropriate.

"That's an awful thing to even suggest, Matthew. He might be really self-conscious about that. That could be his thorn in the flesh."

"His what?"

"His fleshly thorn; it's in the Bible." Mom flipped through her navy blue King James Bible, the only Bible Pastor Nolan approved for the people at IBBC. "The apostle Paul wrote about it in his letter to the, um…" Her voice trailed off as she tried to remember if Paul had written about his personal thorn to the people of Corinth or Thessalonica. She searched her Bible, putting her finger down in random spots and running it across the pages like she was reading Braille. "Or did he mention it in one of his letters to Timothy? Virgil, do you remember?" She looked at my father, who had one hand on the steering wheel and the other hanging out the window, randomly pointing at people he knew or thought he knew. *"Virgil?"*

"Did *who* mention *what*?" asked my father, oblivious to the conversation happening a foot away from his ear.

"Didn't you hear anything we were talking about? Matthew thinks Pastor Nolan doesn't have a neck!"

"Well, he doesn't have much of a neck," said my father. "I thought it was because he wore big collars, but then I saw the boy in a T-shirt. No neck."

"I *know* that," said my mother slowly, talking through her teeth, only moving her lips slightly. She did this amateur ventriloquist act because she didn't want me to know that she wondered the same thing. My mother wasn't fond of exposing weaknesses in front of her kids. This was especially true on Sundays.

"I was trying to explain to Matthew that maybe, on the

remote chance the preacher actually does lack a neck"—she looked at me—"and I'm not saying he does. But if that were true, it could be his personal thorn. You know, something that might torment him when he's alone, looking in the mirror. It's not polite to mock somebody's spiritual burden. I certainly wouldn't want somebody mocking mine."

"Oh, it's hardly his thorn in the flesh, hon," my father said, looking at my mother with the same look he gave foreigners who ran gas stations when they asked if he wanted paper or plastic. "It's not like the man is incapable of turning his head. You're making him sound like a cripple. His chin just sits too close to his shoulders. But he doesn't need healing."

"I wasn't suggesting he was a cripple." My mother sighed audibly. "I only brought you into the conversation because I thought you might remember where the apostle Paul mentioned his thorn in Scripture. I guess I should have kept my mouth closed."

My father stuck his hand back out the window and pointed at some old man who was fat, shirtless, and mowing his lawn. Mom suddenly became interested in the cornfields on her side.

Melanie piped up. "We just came from church!"

"And," said Mom, "what's that supposed to mean?"

"Well, it means we shouldn't be arguing about God after we just left *God's* house."

Nobody said anything for a few minutes.

"So, can I ask one more question?" I stuck my head

between my parents' shoulders again. "Did the apostle Paul have a neck or not?"

My mother looked at me. It wasn't a mean look, just the kind that assured me the apostle Paul indeed had a neck and mine was in jeopardy if I didn't sit back and stop asking questions.

Our Sundays felt different after we joined Pastor Nolan's flock. It wasn't simply the sermons and the people that changed, but to me, God seemed to be changing. I didn't have him all figured out at the time, but one thing I did notice about the new God we worshiped: he followed us home.

Easy Like
Sunday Morning

If a fundamentalist's life could be summed up in a quote, it would be this: "This world is not my home, I'm just passin' through."

I don't know who said it first, but to a lot of people at IBBC, those words offered just enough hope and inspiration for them to muddle through another *blah* day and inch another one closer to Glory.

Gettin' to Glory was what our lives were all about.

The way we saw things, it didn't matter that God had created the heavens and the earth—he did not want us excited about living here. A good fundamentalist worth his weight in guilt was quick to remind any skeptic that the world was going to hell in a handbasket.

As a church, we could only watch as the world burned. God didn't want us wasting our time trying to help things get better. Jesus was coming back! To *save* us from earth's misery.

He wanted our hearts and minds set on what was to come, not rummaging through what we were leaving behind.

Planet earth was just a waiting area, a type of holding cell. Pastor Nolan told us to be patient while we sat in the waiting room and to do our best to avoid reading the magazines and playing with the toys in the plastic toy chest. All we could do was pray, read our Bibles, and wait until our names got called or Jesus came back to rescue us.

To make the time go faster, we sat around and dreamed about heaven.

Heaven was the only true hope for a fundamentalist. The mansions, the gold streets, the pearly gates. Feathers. Those were things worth living for. Once we got to heaven, Pastor Nolan promised, we would be rewarded for how much we hated living on earth.

But heaven required a ticket.

I had only been a Baptist for eight weeks when I got mine—the *first* time. I sat in a very plain Sunday school classroom, listening to my father teach a lesson about Job and trying to decide whether or not I was going to fess up to being a sinner.

My father's classroom was actually the lobby of the Board of Education building. It was more or less just a wide hallway lined with pictures of white men who put my county on the map or aided in keeping it from being removed. Monday through Saturday the hallway functioned as a seating area with magazines and a filing cabinet or two, but on Sundays all of that was cleared away and folding chairs were set up.

That morning my father managed to slip out of the house without my mother noticing he was dressed like a man who sold discount mattresses. The suit he wore was made of a brown plaid material that shimmered a golden hue whenever he stood in direct sunlight or next to a lamp. I think he liked that old three-piece because my mother hated it. Every time he put it on, a fight would erupt in our house.

"Virgil Turner," Mom would say. "Why have you put on that ugly suit again? I swear, you look like the dickens. I don't want to walk out of this house with you looking like that."

"What?" My father always acted as though he was hearing my mother's frustration for the very first time.

"You know very well *what*," Mom would say and then look at whoever else was in the room and throw her hands in the air as if she'd once again come to the realization that she hadn't married one of the men modeling in the JCPenney catalog. "I don't know what I'm going to do with him. Can you believe he intends to go to church dressed like that? He wears the same clothes over and over again. I've been telling him for *years* that he needs to go buy new clothes, but do you think he'll do it?"

"I can't afford new clothes."

"Oh, Virgil." And then Mom rolled her eyes and walked out of the room as if the editors of *GQ* were watching and *smiling*.

It was always the same argument. By the time I was born, my parents had reached a place in their marriage where they no longer needed originality in their tiffs. This particular battle had become almost charming, though completely unfashionable. Dad did look ridiculous dressed in a suit that glistened, but he didn't care. While I always vocalized my support for my mother because it made me feel edgy and cool to be a proponent of high fashion, I secretly cheered Dad on too. He was only being himself, and I suppose he wanted that to be good enough.

There were times when I envied my father for having the right personality to be a Baptist. He was stubborn, could be close-minded toward anything that wasn't his idea, and was fully convinced that Pentecostals were a bunch of nut jobs. Fundamentalism fit my father like a tailored straitjacket. Pursuing God through self-discipline came naturally to him. He didn't seem to mind measuring preaching in decibels, and to him, building a church with old-fashioned business principles made sense. Dad found something in our church that gave him hope.

Regardless of where it comes from, someone else's hope is difficult to devalue.

With the desire that his Sunday school class might learn something biblically profound, my father always added his own story into the lessons he taught. Dad could take the most unbelievable Bible stories and relate them to his life as a child on a farm. On that morning, he'd managed to relate the life of Job to that of Brighteyes, his favorite cow.

"When I was a farm boy," he said, "there wasn't one cow more faithful than Brighteyes. It didn't matter what I put that cow through, she was a faithful and gentle cow. Sometimes I would jump from the rafters of the barn onto the back of Brighteyes, and do you know what she did? She hardly balked. She just carried me out of the barn as calmly as she possibly could. Brighteyes was faithful, and God wants us to be faithful people."

That made sense to me. Sure, God put Job through a lot more torture than Brighteyes experienced and she was a mammal that didn't mind stepping in her own manure, but the comparison worked for our eager class.

Each week, after he'd finished telling us the Bible story, Dad felt obligated to share the plan of salvation.

"Boys and girls, the Bible tells us in Romans 3, verse 23"—Dad began folding his notes and putting them in the front flap of his Bible—"that all of us have sinned, including each and every one of us in this room, and fallen short of the glory of God. I have sinned. You have sinned. And our sin has consequences. The book of Romans also tells us that the *wages* for our sin is death. *Death.*"

Before that day, I'd never thought of myself as a sinner. My mother had never called me a sinner—at least, she never used that exact word to my face. Perhaps it's what she mumbled whenever she caught me pinching my little sister, but she never looked at me and yelled, "Sinner, go to your room."

But I was behind the rest of my Sunday school class. Most

of them had already owned up to being depraved and disgusting. Every week since I'd become a Baptist, I'd witnessed other children my age admitting they were sinners before God and man.

Most of the kids I knew realized they were sinners before they were old enough to understand they were human. For instance, a kid named Leonard confessed to hating his mother on occasion. He just blurted it out one Sunday. It was unclear to me whether he was making a confession to God or suffering from Tourette's—perhaps a variety that came with a conscience.

"Sinners need to ask Jesus into their hearts," my father said.

I glanced at Ally, the wealthiest kid in our church. If there was anybody in my class who needed Jesus to come and live inside her body—no doubt in a mansion—it was Ally. She didn't seem capable of repenting from sin and had a severe problem with bragging. If she wasn't trying to get me to touch her rabbit-fur coat, she was throwing her leather-bound Bible in my face to smell. "Doesn't it smell good? It's not synthetic like yours. My mother said it was very expensive." Even though she was only five and a half, she was like a kindergarten version of a televangelist.

When I got older, I decided that upon arriving in heaven, I would ask God to do me a favor and *not* put my mansion close to Ally's. I assumed he'd already know my reasons for making such a request. He'd know how tempted she would be to come over to my mansion and boast about how nicely

furnished her house was compared to mine. She would pretend to be coming over to borrow an egg or a cup of sugar,
but once she was there she'd make comments. "Oh, God gave
you the *copper* entranceway? I'm sorry. He made my gates
pearly. And they are just divine."

While I didn't want to be neighbors with Ally, I wanted
her to make the cut, hoping Jesus might make being her
friend on this side a little easier.

As I listened to my father's talk, I wondered if I needed to
ask Jesus into my heart too.

That's how people became Christians at my church. We
invited Jesus to live inside our chest cavities. At the time, I
thought it sounded like a painful procedure, one that might
involve a shot or stitches. I didn't like pain or blood. I was still
at an age when I tried to avoid bowel movements at all costs,
so I wasn't sure I wanted the Son of God building a condo
inside one of my atriums.

I did learn one thing about having Jesus as a bodily ten-
ant: he would not tolerate cigarette smoke. Mr. Parsons, the
assistant pastor in charge of children's ministries, made that
perfectly clear. "Do you want to give Jesus *cancer*?" His voice
was gruff and he put his hands on his hips. "*Well,* do you?
Think about it, young people. Do you want to be the person
responsible for giving God's Son cancer? Or how about
emphysema?" After his talk, Mr. Parsons stood at the door,
shook our hands, and gave us Hershey bars.

Jesus didn't mind getting fat.

My father ended his talk with a question, one he said was *very* important. "Would anyone in this room like to ask Jesus into your heart? If so, all you have to do is raise your hand and somebody will help you do that. Anybody at all?"

One person raised his hand—Michael, the only black kid at IBBC until our church started a children's bus ministry three years later. When Michael stood up, everybody looked at him. Michael was two years older than me. On that morning, he looked very astute in his gray suit and wire-framed glasses. "I'd like to do it, Mr. Turner."

"That's great, son." My father grinned. "Glad you've decided to make this decision. It will change your life in so many wonderful ways. You just wait."

Maybe I wanted my father to grin at me the same way he had grinned at Michael, or maybe I really did think I was a sinner. Either way, as soon as Michael headed toward the back of the room, I raised my hand.

"I want to do it too," I said. "I want to ask Jesus into my heart."

Upon hearing the high-pitched squeal of my voice, my father smiled bigger than I'd ever seen him before.

"You do, Buck? That's wonderful."

"Are you nervous, Matthew?" asked Mr. Davis, the Sunday school volunteer assigned to implant Jesus into Michael and me while my father managed the rest of the class.

"Yes sir. A little."

"Don't be nervous. Asking Jesus into your heart is easy. There's nothing to it. No reason to be scared."

Mr. Davis's tone reminded me of television doctors or dentists who said things like, "I'm going to remove your tonsils now," or, "I need to fill this one cavity." But he said it with confidence, like he'd performed this particular procedure successfully thousands of times, so his words did make me feel less anxious.

Mr. Davis led us out of the classroom and into a stairwell that smelled like mothballs and old cinderblocks.

"We'll talk in here, boys. We'll be able to hear better. What you're getting ready to do is far too important for you not to be able to hear, huh?"

Mr. Davis nodded his head and smiled awkwardly. That was something I'd seen adults do when they hadn't spent much time around kids or were trying too hard to fit in. He fumbled through the pages of his Bible, mumbling to himself, "Ugh, that's not what I'm looking for. Where in the world is that verse?"

I had to concentrate very hard not to stare at the small wart on Mr. Davis's forehead. Warts in visible places made the hairs on the back of my neck jiggle. Michael broke the silence. "Mr. Davis, do you have a job?"

"Of course, I have a job." He glanced at Michael over the rims of his glasses. "How do you think I live?"

"I don't know," said Michael. "I hadn't really thought about it. What do you do?"

"I sell insurance, Michael. Life, health, and sometimes

vehicle insurance." He put his finger on a spot in his Bible. "You guys will have to call me in about fifteen years when you need insurance. But until then, let's set you up with a different kind of life insurance policy."

He read a verse from the Bible, one that reminded Michael and me that we were sinners.

"This next verse, here"—I noticed Mr. Davis was sucking on a mint—"*this* verse proves that all of us were *born* enemies of God. *Enemies*. Crazy, huh? What that verse says is that without Jesus, God doesn't like any of us all that much."

Even though some of what Mr. Davis said about God seemed mean—some bordered on violent—his words didn't seem nearly as combative when combined with the minty-fresh scent of wintergreen.

"Do you have another mint?" I asked.

Mr. Davis looked at me over the frames of his reading glasses. "I don't have another mint." He smiled. "I'm sorry. Somebody else gave me this mint."

He started reading again.

"Mr. Davis," I said, "do you think the person who gave you that mint has two more for Michael and me?" I looked at Michael to see if he agreed. He nodded.

"I don't know," said Mr. Davis.

"Well, would you mind asking them?"

"Matthew, do you see anyone else in this room?"

"I thought we could go find them."

"No. I think that can wait."

"But we're hungry."

"You're going to wait ten minutes, Matthew!"

"Oh," I said, disappointed. I crossed my arms and stared at the fire extinguisher hanging in the corner.

"We're in the middle of something important. You'll be fine, Matthew. I promise."

He only thought that because he already had a mint.

Mr. Davis read several more verses from Romans.

"It says right here that Jesus died for your sins and his blood makes you clean. Isn't that good news? Once you accept him as your personal Savior, you are no longer a slave to sin or sentenced to an eternity in hell. You are set free. You guys don't want to go to hell, do you?"

Michael and I shook our heads. Who in their right mind wanted to go to hell? I hated being sent to my room. An eternity in my room would have killed me. After twenty-seven minutes of solitary confinement, I began making up imaginary friends, celebrities who could get me on *Star Search* or *Sesame Street*. I hated being alone. And hell sounded lonely.

Mr. Davis asked Michael and me to bow our heads, close our eyes, and repeat whatever he said. The two of us echoed Mr. Davis's prayer.

The whole ordeal was simple, really, much less complicated than I expected. In the same time it took to microwave a bag of popcorn, Mr. Davis helped Michael and me secure our escape route from hell.

"It's that easy, guys," he said, shaking each of our hands.

"Welcome to the family of God. You both are now held in the arms of Jesus."

"Jesus is holding me?" Michael asked.

"Yep, and he'll never let go," said Mr. Davis.

"I don't feel anybody's arms around me," I said.

"Well, it's not something you would actually *feel,* Matthew; it's more like something you would sense. You'll understand it in time."

"So he's living inside my heart, and he's also able to hug me on the outside?" I asked.

"Jesus can do anything."

"Oh."

"I am very proud of you both. It's hard to believe I'm looking at two brand-new creatures! According to the apostle Paul, all of your desires have now changed. You should no longer need or want the things you did just ten minutes ago. That's the miracle of salvation."

I wanted to believe that was true. I wanted to know beyond any doubt that something truly miraculous had just happened, but maybe nothing changed, because I still really wanted a mint.

"Matthew and Michael, go find your parents and tell them the good news," said Mr. Davis excitedly. "Tell them that you are a new creation and that Jesus is living in your heart."

"Thank you, Mr. Davis," I said.

If I'm honest, the best part of that day for me wasn't

Jesus's new home in my heart. My mother's reaction was the best part.

When she heard the news, she was speechless. Tears formed in her eyes, and the hug she gave me seemed to last forever. It was tangible. Real hope shined in her eyes because something extraordinary had happened, something I was incapable of comprehending that day. Mom's embrace I understood. It meant something to me, more than what I experienced in the stairwell.

"Matthew Turner was one of two boys who asked Jesus into their hearts this morning," said Pastor Nolan during the announcements at church. "Four years old! Wow. I wish I'd known Jesus when I was four. Imagine what kind of Christian he's going to be when he becomes an adult. Can't wait to see that."

For the people in my church, the day you realized you were a sinner was a very good day. A day to celebrate, one to write down in your Bible and remember for years to come. Pastor Nolan told us that all the angels in heaven threw a big party on that day. "They pull out streamers and noisemakers," he shouted. "And maybe even some sparkling grape juice— the nonalcoholic kind, of course—and they have a huge celebration in your honor. All of heaven is aglow."

I once asked Pastor Nolan if he thought any of the angels danced during the celebration.

"No, Matthew," he said. "Angels don't dance when they get excited. That would make them demons."

"The Bible says King David danced."

"He probably skipped or galloped or something."

"Well, maybe the angels skip."

"They might skip, but not seductively."

The angels skipped—*modestly*—a lot for me during my childhood because I asked Jesus into my heart often. It happened anytime Pastor Nolan preached about hell, the Tribulation, or communist China. And once when he mentioned Barbara Mandrell and the Mandrell Sisters. Sometimes I did it just to be sure I wasn't going to hell. Other times it happened because I felt scared, and asking Jesus into my heart numbed my fear until the next sermon on the End Times.

Sitting in the waiting room got boring sometimes, so inviting Jesus into my heart every now and again helped. I can understand why all of us got so excited about *just passin' through*.

Haircut

I was going to the barbershop because Jesus hated little boys who had long hair.

"Long hair on a woman is glorifying to God, but on a man it's an abomination," Pastor Nolan preached the day before. My father came home from the Sunday service not wanting Jesus to disapprove of anything I did.

At breakfast, he had looked at my mother and, sounding serious, said, "Hon, I think it's time Matthew got a real haircut. You know, at the barbershop where I go."

Mom looked at my head.

"Don't you think it's time to get that mop of his cut? Look at it. It sort of makes him look like a girl."

My ears perked and my stomach gurgled. *A girl?* I thought. *He didn't think I looked like a girl three months ago.* But three months ago we had been Methodist. I put a spoonful of Cheerios in my mouth and waited for Mom to save the day. She always saved the day—or at least made us believe she had.

Things went differently now that we were fundamentalists.

Instead of coming to the rescue of my chin-length locks, Mom just sat there looking at Dad. She didn't argue with him, even though I'm pretty sure she wanted to. The corners of her mouth were turned slightly downward—a sure sign she was thinking about the conversation and considering her chances of winning this argument.

The stress was killing me. It was the kind of stress that made it impossible to enjoy whole milk.

"Mom, why can't you cut my hair?" I put my fists underneath either side of my chin. "I like you cutting my hair."

Mom directed her raised eyebrows at my father and then looked back at me. "Aw, baby, Mommy isn't very good at cutting hair."

"I think you're good."

"But I don't have the right tools to cut your hair like the church requires." She looked at me and smiled. "It takes more than a pair of scissors to get your hair short enough for God. A barber will have to do that."

"Can you at least try?"

"I would make a mess of your head, Matthew. That haircut is hard enough with the right tools. It would be impossible for me."

"And you want it done right, Buck." Dad turned his fork upside down and stabbed a sausage link. "This is important. Weren't you listening to Pastor Nolan yesterday?"

I had heard him. It was impossible not to hear Pastor Nolan's sermons. He didn't simply tell us what God wanted us to do, he screamed the messages at us. Sometimes he yelled his sermons so loudly Mom wondered if he was hard of hearing or if he thought we were. During his sermon the day before, when he told us what Jesus thought about longhaired hippies, rock stars, and John Travolta, he had gotten so loud that the church's sound system crackled with feedback.

"A man's hair should be tapered up the sides and in the back," Pastor Nolan exclaimed, beating one of his fists against the pulpit. "In other words, he should look like a man. While I'm on the subject, let me say this: there are a lot of liberal preachers in this country who would love for you to believe that Jesus had long hair. I'm here to tell you that's a barefaced lie. Nothing burns me up more than when I see artwork that makes *my* Lord and Savior look like a fruitcake or a homosexual. You can be sure of this, people—there was nothing remotely feminine about Jesus. He was all man."

Pastor Nolan only approved of one picture of Jesus. It was a simple picture, one artist's rendering that depicted six little kids all happily trying to jump onto the lap of a man who looked exactly like Tom Selleck in a Hilton Suites bathrobe. In the picture, Jesus had the most peculiar grin on his face. But some people didn't even like that picture. They thought the way Jesus was grinning was unnatural for the Savior of the world. Furthermore, a couple of the third-grade girls weren't sure if their moms would want them sitting in the lap of a Jesus who looked like Magnum, P.I., preparing for a warm bath.

"Look at my hair." Pastor Nolan spun around and showed us the back of his head.

"This is how Jesus wants a man's hair to look. Can I get an amen?"

My father said amen. By this time, my father was a deacon, and one of the main responsibilities of a deacon was making sure Pastor Nolan's request for an amen never went unanswered. Eventually, Dad's ability to answer Pastor Nolan became a natural reflex. Sometimes he had no idea what he was agreeing with, so after saying amen, he'd look at my mother and ask, "What did he just say?"

My mother picked up her piece of toast and took a small bite. "Matthew, here's the deal. Your father and I want to do the right thing. We want God to be pleased with how we're raising you. So let's do this the right way."

"That settles it. You're getting a haircut." My father looked at me with the kind of conviction that's reserved for Supreme Court cases. "I'll take you this afternoon."

"Yes sir," I said nervously. I stood up from the table and took my cereal bowl to the sink.

My stomach still gurgling, I ran to the bathroom.

As my father took a seat in the barbershop's waiting area, he grabbed an old copy of *American Hunter* from the shelf and began reading a story about how to properly kill black bears with a bow and arrow.

"Gosh, I would love to do that some time. Hachoo boy, that looks like fun."

I had a hard time choosing a seat, but eventually decided to sit three seats to the left of my father. Sitting next to him didn't bother me. But walking through the barbershop's front door, I became enthralled with the twirling red and white candy cane hanging outside right next to the neon Open sign. I wanted to watch it.

"Virgil, you just here for a haircut?" My father's barber, Mr. Harry, had a raspy voice. It sounded like the kind of voice that spent all day fermenting in his esophagus. Each time he said something, I felt this strange need to clear my throat.

"No, Harry. My son, Matthew, is getting his first *real* haircut today."

"Oh really?" Mr. Harry stood on his tippytoes so he could look at me over the counter. "So, you're here for your first real haircut?"

I didn't say anything. Not because I was trying to be rude, but because the candy cane had hypnotized me. I sat there, trying my hardest to figure out where the stripes went after they had twirled down to the bottom. They seemed to just disappear, but I knew that was impossible.

When I heard the distinct sound of my father clearing his throat, I looked up at him.

"Mr. Harry is talking to you. He wants to know why you're here."

"I'm here because Jesus doesn't like men having long hair, and my hair is long."

My father's face turned into a slight grin behind his magazine. I knew that grin. The same one appeared when he watched me shoot my BB gun for the first time. He was proud of how I had answered Mr. Harry's question.

To my father, this haircut was much more than doing away with my Bobby Brady mop. It was about me *looking* like a Baptist. I think my father thought the angels in heaven would be a good bit happier once my head looked as clean-cut as a marine's.

"So Jesus only likes short hair, does he?" Mr. Harry smirked.

At the time, I didn't fully understand sarcasm, but it was obvious Mr. Harry didn't love Jesus. Not the way I did. For one thing, he slouched. Pastor Nolan told us that a man's posture said a lot about his character. All the men at church stood up straight. I did too. Every time I saw Pastor Nolan at church, I pretended to be a soldier—a tall one, with a gun and a whole slew of badges. He would walk by me like he was a king inspecting his knights, and if he approved, he would pat my head and say, "You're a good kid, Matthew."

Which was true, I believed.

"Well, I'll be with you in just a couple of minutes, Matthew," said Mr. Harry, who was cutting the hair of a man who looked strikingly similar to Boss Hogg from *The Dukes of Hazzard*. I instantly decided I would refer to him as "Hogg—the hairiest man I had ever seen." In order to make

Hogg look more civilized, Mr. Harry pulled out his clippers and began buzzing Hogg's hair like he was shearing a sheep. In a matter of minutes, Hogg walked out the barber's front door looking almost as clean-cut as televangelist Jimmy Swaggart. My mother enjoyed watching Pastor Swaggart on television on Sunday evenings, but she wasn't allowed to talk about her admiration for Jimmy around anyone at church because he was one of those "tongues speakers," as Dad put it. Pastor Nolan said tongues speakers would lead us astray.

Mr. Harry waved good-bye to Hogg through the window. "You ready for that haircut, Matthew? You can have a seat right here, young man." He pointed to his barber's chair.

Mr. Harry's barber's chair seemed like it had been made for a fat man. When sitting on my bottom, I could only see the top of my forehead in the mirror. Mr. Harry put a booster underneath my backside, which put me a good six inches higher, and then he spun me like a merry-go-round.

"Okay, *Dad.*" Mr. Harry looked at me. "How does *Jesus* want this boy's hair cut?"

"Short," said Dad seriously. "Make it *very* short."

Both Dad and Mr. Harry looked at me in the mirror as they spoke about my hair. Peering at someone through the reflection of a mirror makes things very different. They spoke as if I wasn't even there, like they were looking right through my thinly framed body instead of at me.

"I want it *tapered* on the sides and in the back," said Dad, repeating our pastor's words.

"Tapered," said Mr. Harry, like he knew exactly what

Dad was talking about. "So, I'm giving the boy the 'Baptist church' cut." He chuckled. "Why didn't you say that, Virgil?"

"I guess I didn't know it had a name."

Mr. Harry put a barber's cape around my neck and tied it tightly. I liked the cape. As soon as it was tied, I instantly became Robin from *Batman*. Robin was my favorite. He seemed much friendlier than Batman, and he was little like I was. The cape ignited my imagination. Inside my head, I wasn't getting a haircut, I was helping Batman save Gotham City from the evil Joker. Jumping off buildings, soaring through the air, and beating up bad guys was easy to imagine while wearing my trusty cobalt blue barber's cape. Despite having a two-inch hole in its bottom seam, I declared it bulletproof, absolutely impenetrable. Nothing could stop me. For as long as it would take Mr. Harry to cut my hair, I planned on being busy as a caped crusader bringing order, justice, and peace to Gotham.

But then I felt something hit my neck.

Hair!

My own cut hair had managed to burn through my cape's protective seal and get beneath my shirt and hit my skin.

It itched.

I scratched.

Joker got me.

As Mr. Harry cut, the *burr* of his clippers tickled my eardrums. The clippers felt good against my skull too. All in all, I was enjoying my trip to the barber. Everything smelled manly. Even Mr. Harry's hands. Anytime his fingers grazed near my nose, I'd catch a whiff of old skin and Brut cologne.

Mr. Harry cut hair fast, much faster than my mom cut my hair. And he seemed to know this particular haircut quite well.

"The men at your church keep me in business," he joked. "Even your pastor comes to see me. Which reminds me, Virgil—your reverend tried to convert me to Baptist a few weeks ago." Mr. Harry let out a gut-filled laugh.

"Oh yeah?" Dad was only moderately interested, not nearly enough to divert him from learning how to kill bears with a bow and arrow.

"Yep, he talks to me about Jesus nearly every time he comes in here. I guess he thinks I'm going to hell," he said, still smirking and slouching. "He keeps talking to me about becoming born again. Born again! Ha! But the last time he came in here, I went ahead and set him straight. You want to know what I said?"

"What did you say, Harry?" I could tell Dad wanted Mr. Harry to shut up.

"I told him, 'Reverend, I *am* born again. I reckon I'm a born-again heathen.'" Mr. Harry laughed so loud I nearly fell out of the barber's chair. "Virgil, your preacher got the funniest look on his face. It cracked me up."

Mr. Harry stopped laughing.

"But then I looked at him, and I told him, 'Pastor Nolan, I cut hair. I don't want your religion. I don't believe in all that religious—'"

Right after he said the word *religious,* Mr. Harry said a word I had never heard spoken before. It started with the letter *s* and rhymed with "pit." Even though I didn't know what it meant, it was obvious from the look of panic on my father's face that it was a word I wasn't supposed to know about until I became much older, and even then, I would only be allowed to think it.

As soon as Mr. Harry said the *s* word, everything became quiet in the barbershop. My father's expression put my mind on lockdown. I closed my eyes and started praying, *Help me, Jesus; help me, Jesus; help me, Jesus.* My mother said I should always pray as soon as I felt the need to. She told me that prayer helped Jesus protect me. I believed that. As soon as my ears heard the *s* word, Jesus jumped off his heavenly throne, rushed over to my heart's front door, and locked it tight.

If Jesus is protecting me, he must hate Mr. Harry, I thought. I began picturing God sitting on his throne in heaven, looking down on the barbershop, and shaking his head in disgust at Mr. Harry. I always pictured God having a scary voice, like the wizard from *The Wizard of Oz.* I imagined God yelling, *"Mr. Harry! You know it makes me angry to hear you use that word! You'll burn for that one."*

Obviously Mr. Harry didn't care, since he interrupted God's judgment by spinning the barber chair in my father's direction. "Voilà. How's this, Virgil? Short enough?"

"Looks good to me, Harry," said Dad.

Upon getting the thumbs-up from Dad, Mr. Harry

brushed me off with what he said was a horsehair brush. Then he took off the cape and helped me out of the chair.

"How do you like your Jesus cut, Matthew?"

I stood on my tippytoes and looked in the big mirror. I turned to both sides and looked at my reflection out of the corner of my eye.

"My ears look big." I looked at Dad. I had never really seen my ears before, and they looked huge. I swore Mr. Harry had made them grow.

"Your ears look fine." Dad pulled his wallet out of his back pocket.

"You don't think my ears look big?" I asked.

"Son, your ears look like ears. *They're fine.*"

"Will Mom think my ears look big? When she cuts my hair, my ears never look big." My father wasn't the kind of man who had the time or the patience to worry about things like ears, but Mom did. She would definitely tell me if my ears had gotten bigger.

"Your mother will not notice your ears, Matthew. I think you look fine. Let's pay and get out of here."

My father handed Mr. Harry a five-dollar bill; he followed Dad and me outside.

"I guess I'll see you guys next time," he said as we jumped into the truck. As Dad pulled out of the parking spot, I watched Mr. Harry take out a pack of cigarettes and place one between his lips. My eyes got big, and my mouth dropped open as he lit up.

"Dad! Mr. Harry smokes!"

Dad didn't say anything.

But I felt sorry for Mr. Harry all the way home, worrying about him going to hell.

When we arrived, I ran into the house. Mom was in the kitchen.

"Wow, look at you," she said, drying her hands with the World's Greatest Mom apron tied around her waist. "My little boy looks like a Christian soldier now."

She smiled and kissed my cheeks at least twenty times, ran her fingers through my lack of hair, and gave me a hug. I grinned. I was so excited Mom liked my haircut that I completely forgot to tell her about Mr. Harry's eternal damnation.

"You really do look like a little man now, Matthew," she exclaimed, and then I watched as her expression changed from immense joy to concern. "Virgil." She looked at my father, who had just walked through the door, "Do Matthew's ears look a little big?"

Dad ignored her and kept walking toward the back of the house.

She looked down at me. "Don't worry, honey. That's nothing a little prayer and Scotch tape won't fix!"

Mom always had lots of faith, especially when a brand name was involved.

"The important thing to remember, Matthew, is that sometimes, even when we *obey* Jesus's teachings, life still doesn't turn out the way we expect it to." Mom put her hands on either side of my head and pushed. I think she was trying to flatten my ears down; either that, or she was trying to heal them. "Do you understand what I'm saying?"

"Yeah, I think so."

"What am I saying?"

"You think Jesus made my ears big."

"That's not what I'm saying at all."

"Is it Dad's fault?"

Mom stood up and giggled her way back to the stove.

"Why are you laughing?"

"No reason, son. Just proud of you, that's all."

Twelve Minutes

A few minutes before four o'clock on a Sunday afternoon, Pastor Nolan was due to arrive at our house for an impromptu meeting with my father.

I hated when Pastor Nolan came over.

By the time I was seven, the man whom God had chosen to lead Chestertown to Jesus frightened the hell out of me. *Literally.* Besides the Trinity, hellfire and brimstone were his two favorite things. I was convinced he kept a good supply of both items hidden in one of the church's storage closets for special occasions like Thanksgiving or Easter and just in case the local college ever tried to start a Hanukkah celebration.

For a long time I didn't know what brimstone was, but I pictured it as massive boulders falling like rain from the sky. Anytime Pastor Nolan talked about it, I visualized my best friend, Julie—she was Catholic—trying to outrun one of the boulders in her front yard. Just as the boulder was about to roll over her, I shook myself free of the image. The thought of Julie being judged by God haunted me.

Whenever Pastor Nolan was around, there was reason to worry. He was like a nicer-looking Grim Reaper. His sermons were angry and hopeless, and if hope happened to slip in, it was a footnote. It certainly didn't feel like anything worthy of a highlighter.

Most people in my church thought Pastor Nolan was perfect, that God had made him without flaws. People seemed entranced by him. Even if he had been a sinner like the rest of us, nobody would have noticed. And if they did notice, they would have been too intimidated to bring it up.

For me, that made Pastor Nolan uncomfortable to be around. I didn't think he was going to hurt me, and I managed being in the same room with him as long as other people were there to keep him entertained. But I was convinced that, if he and I ended up in the same room without a chaperon, he would ask me spiritual questions I wouldn't feel comfortable answering.

"How often does your father read his Bible?" I imagined him wanting to know. *"Does your mother kneel or lay prostrate while she's praying? It doesn't really matter—I'm just curious."*

Even though I was known as a talkative kid, I would have become mute under those conditions. I loved my mother and father too much to let them fall victim to one of Pastor Nolan's sermon illustrations.

I also worried Pastor Nolan would ask me to do something impossible. It wasn't the normal, everyday impossible I feared—like putting the toilet seat down or remembering to flush after a number two—it was the *biblical* kind of impossible that scared me. I had visions of him asking me to recite the names of all sixty-six books of the Bible or the Four Spiritual Laws according to the apostle Paul or the thirty-seven manners in which God punished people for disobedience. I also worried he might ask me to demonstrate my own faith in God by seeing if I could walk across our church's baptistery pool. Or at the very least, part it down the middle.

"Moses could do it," he'd say. *"Your faith is kind of puny. That's not good. Are you sure you've asked Jesus into your heart?"*

Then, I figured, he would put his hands on my forehead and pray that God would relieve the devil of his duties in my life.

"Now get back up there and walk across that water. This time...concentrate."

My mother wasn't scared of Pastor Nolan at all, so she loved when he visited. Miraculously, whenever a pastoral visit was on the calendar, my mother turned into June Cleaver. She pulled out the good china, made sure the stereo was set to the hymn-playing station, and instead of speaking in her regular voice, she'd sing-talk.

"Matthew, go put your sneakers in your closet," she'd sing to me like she was auditioning for a part on one of those old-time radio soap operas. My mother had a good singing voice, so her performance was impressive. Talking that way made her sound more sophisticated. She seemed more like the women the church considered good fundamentalist role models, the women who wrote Christian advice columns for the *Sword of the Lord* newspaper. Their columns, tucked into the back of the paper, were usually about "mom" things or submitting to husbands. The experts had names like Mary, Pam, or Esther, and in their pictures wore wide aprons and held Bibles with their cookie-dough-covered hands. Mom would have made an excellent columnist had she not been physically fit.

"Matthew, can you please get the door?" My mother looked at me. "I think Pastor Nolan is here."

I didn't move. I thought about moving. It crossed my mind as soon as I heard my mother's request. But instead of moving, I stood frozen at my mother's side and watched her pull a sheet of cookies out of the oven. I knew I was supposed to be walking to the front door, but I couldn't. The thought of letting Pastor Nolan inside our house had paralyzed me, like the nerves in my body had all decided to take naps at exactly the same time. It felt like one of those temporary comas, maybe something that was going around.

"Matthew, did you hear me?"

As soon as I looked at my mother, she began shooing me over to the door with her head.

"Go let Pastor Nolan in. *Please.* My hands are full."

I walked to the front door. Pastor Nolan's face peered at me through the window, and he waved and smiled. He looked as though he should have been suction-cupped onto the back window of my sister's car, maybe with the words *Smart Girl on Board* etched into his palm.

I turned the deadbolt and opened the door.

"Hey, young man!" Pastor Nolan smiled at me as though he were a really nice person who meant me no harm. "How's Mr. Matthew doing? I think you might have grown an inch or two since I saw you last, little guy."

"That's impossible," I said. "I saw you this morning."

He looked at me and grinned. I imagined it was the same kind of grin my father said opossums had.

"Oh, I'm pretty sure you grew at least an inch."

"Mom." I started backing away from the door. "Pastor Nolan is inside the house. Can you please come and get him?"

I counted to three and then yelled again.

"Mom, did you hear me? Pastor Nolan is *inside* the house. The one we live in! *We're alone at the door!* Mom!"

Pastor Nolan stood patiently on the doormat with his hands crossed, holding his Bible in front of his pants zipper like he was waiting for a soccer ball.

To pass the time, we looked at each other. We didn't talk. Neither of us had anything to say. While looking him up and down, that morning's pre-sermon came to mind. Pre-sermons were four-and-a-half-minute rants that Pastor Nolan added to our church service when we finally got a building with a steeple. He said having a church building with a stage made him feel more like a preacher because it gave him something to jump around on. My grandmother thought that was baloney. I'd heard her tell one of my aunts that she thought he felt more like a preacher because he was eighteen inches higher than everybody else.

During that morning's pre-sermon, Pastor Nolan had whetted our spiritual appetites by talking about how easy it was to see sin in another person's life just by looking in their eyes. For a fundamentalist, spotting sin was like going to Disney World.

"Sometimes I'll see a person on the street," he said, pointing his finger in various directions around the auditorium for emphasis. "And I'll think to myself, 'That man right there is up to no good. He's probably got beer in his fridge. Or he's a smoker! Or he's breaking one of the Ten Commandments!'" He smiled. "Some of you know what I'm talking about. You have the gift too. It's like God gives us a view of a person's life just by looking into their eyes."

I wondered what he was seeing in my life. He had an intense stare. It seemed to penetrate my skin like he was Superman and his x-ray vision was on high alert. The thought occurred to me that he could be scanning my soul for sin. Suddenly, I felt as naked as the people who modeled unmentionables in department store ads. *This is what Adam and Eve felt like in the Garden of Eden,* I thought. I wanted so much to cover up, but my mother didn't keep fig leaves in the house.

■   ■   ■

My father and Pastor Nolan talked in the family room for an hour. I didn't get to hear the conversation, but since Pastor Nolan was carrying his Bible and his fingers were stuck in its pages in four different places, I knew it was a serious talk. Whatever the topic, he had already looked up God's opinion on the matter, and by the looks of it, heaven was planning another Inquisition.

When Pastor Nolan was about to leave, I stood in the kitchen next to my sister Elisabeth. My mother had gathered the entire family together so we could say good-bye to him in unison. She believed that was the polite thing to do when an important person left our home. And there was nobody more important in our lives than Pastor Nolan.

"Pastor's leaving," she sang loudly.

My sisters and I knew that was our cue to bounce into the kitchen, smiles on our faces, like we did this sort of thing all the time. Every time we did it, I couldn't help but be reminded of that scene from *The Sound of Music* when Captain von Trapp, Maria, and the kids sing good-bye in four-part harmony to their party guests.

As Pastor Nolan shook Elisabeth's hand, I wanted to be singing, "Adieu, adieu, to yieu and yieu and yieu," and then prepare to escape the Third Reich waiting for me in the living room.

When it was my turn to say good-bye, Pastor Nolan got down on one knee in front of me and put his hands on my shoulders. *Great,* I thought. *He's going to tell my mother about the sin he sees in my life and out me for the seven-year-old fraud he believes I am.*

"Matthew, how would you like to drive with me to Sunday evening church?" he asked.

Before I had a chance to shake my head, my mother piped up. "I think that's a fantastic idea. He would love that, Preacher." She looked at me with eyes that assured me I would indeed *love it* or else. "*Wouldn't you love that,* Matthew?"

"Yes ma'am," I said, lying. I felt guilty about lying, but it was either that or risk disappointing Pastor Nolan and irritating my mother. Mom wanted her children to love Pastor Nolan as much as she did.

My older sisters did. At our church's annual Pastor Appreciation Day, they joined together with eight or nine other teenage girls, stood in front of the entire church, and sang, "We love you, Preacher. Oh yes, we do. We don't love anyone as much as you. When you're not with us, we're blue. Oh, Preacher, we love you." Each of them seemed to have a schoolgirl crush on him. When they finished singing, they presented him with a huge card and baked goods. He was like a celebrity in their eyes. More popular than the two guys who played cops on *CHiPs*.

That's why my mother got so excited about me riding with Pastor Nolan in his Corolla. It was an opportunity she didn't want me to refuse. But Pastor Nolan didn't make her nervous like he made me.

．．．

Twelve minutes, I thought. *I can survive twelve minutes.* That was how long it took my father to drive to church, and he drove ten miles below the speed limit. With any luck, Pastor Nolan would at least drive the speed limit, and that would get us to church in ten minutes, maybe less. My time alone with him would be about the same amount of time it took an episode of *I Love Lucy* to get to its first commercial break. That's how I deciphered time—by thinking about it in terms of half-hour sitcoms.

School was thirteen sitcoms long. Church was three. Baking a cake was a little more than one. For some reason—perhaps because I could replay most episodes of *I Love Lucy* in my mind—the length of a sitcom seemed much more tolerable than minutes.

As we turned out of my driveway toward town, Pastor Nolan did exactly what I was afraid he was going to do. He talked to me.

"So"—Pastor Nolan swallowed hard—"tell me something about your life, Matthew."

"What do you mean?" I asked, crossing my arms so I would appear less interested. My mother accidentally taught me that.

"Aw, you know what I mean. Tell me something about yourself that I don't already know."

"Like what?"

"Anything. Like, what have you been learning about God lately?"

"You already know what I've learned about God."

"Why is that?"

"You're the preacher. You know everything."

"I know everything?" Pastor Nolan glanced over at me and smiled. I think he might have gotten goose bumps from hearing somebody say that out loud. "Oh, I don't know everything, Matthew. But thanks for thinking that I do. Can I talk to you about something?"

Uh-oh. He was going to ask me to provide evidence for my faith. He'd probably ask me to move a mountain or a house or a stop sign using only my belief in God. And when I wouldn't be able to do it, he'd pull out Aaron's rod—the one that budded—and do it himself and make me look bad in front of my guardian angel.

I knew I was incapable of moving mountains with my faith. I had tried that summer when my mother and father took me on my first camping trip to the Appalachian Mountains in Virginia. As soon as the mountains popped up over the horizon on Highway 66, I began testing the abilities of my faith by commanding mountain after mountain to move.

"I have faith, I have faith, I have faith, I have faith," I repeated over and over again, something I'd seen a black preacher do on television. He hadn't moved a mountain, but he did make a woman's diabetes disappear. Since it worked for him, I figured it might work for me. When I was really certain that I possessed the necessary faith, I pointed my finger at the mountain of choice and yelled, "MOVE, MOUNTAIN, MOVE!" I did this about thirty times. On one occasion I thought I'd made one of the mountains disappear, which got me very excited, since I thought that might be even better than making one move. But after bragging about it to my father, it reappeared a mile later.

After that camping trip, I told my Sunday school teacher, Mrs. Snover, what had happened. The next week she brought in a small container of mustard seeds to show me how small my faith really was.

"You know what this means, Matthew, right?" she said as she sprinkled several mustard seeds into the palm of my hand. "According to the words of Jesus, your faith is smaller than one of these. We almost need a microscope to see it. Yours is like a molecule."

"So can I ask you about something?" Pastor Nolan asked me, interrupting my thoughts. His voice sounded nervous, which was proof for me that he was actually a human being.

"I guess that's okay," I said. "My grandmother says people should ask more questions. She thinks questions help the world spin around. She also believes people learn from asking questions. So you can ask."

I prepared for the kind of question I was sure would give me stomach ulcers.

"Matthew." Pastor Nolan pulled a necktie off the rearview mirror as he spoke. It was dark brown with a cross and an empty tomb painted on the wide end. The art was clearly amateur, since the empty tomb looked more like a freshly baked loaf of bread than whatever a tomb was suppose to look like. "I'm going to baptize people next Sunday, and I wondered if you would like to be one of them."

My eyes got big.

"My father told you, didn't he?" I yelped. "That I'm scared to get baptized. Did he tell you why? He did, didn't he?"

"Yeah, your father mentioned you were a little scared," he said, taking both his hands off the steering wheel, flipping up his collar, and tossing his tie around his shirt. "But he didn't tell me why. You want to tell me?"

It became difficult to concentrate on the conversation when Pastor Nolan didn't put his hands back on the steering wheel. Instead, he began tying a knot into his tie. He'd obviously forgotten he was driving a car and, more importantly, that I hadn't yet lived to see third grade.

"Pastor Nolan, there's a sharp curve coming up in a little bit."

"I know," he said, looking at his handiwork in the rearview mirror.

"Don't you think you'd better put your hands back on the steering wheel?"

He crossed the wide end of the tie over the thin end and then flipped it through the middle. As the sharp curve got closer, Pastor Nolan didn't flinch. The car just kept heading straight toward the ditch.

"Pastor Nolan!" I yelled as loud as I could. "The curve!"

"Oh, ye of little faith, Matthew," he said, sliding his perfect knot up to the top button of his shirt and folding his collar down. He licked one of his fingers and used it to pat down a couple of sideburn hairs sticking straight out. He checked his nostrils like he was on a tour of Luray Caverns.

I screamed like a girl. "Pastor Nolan, please grab the steering wheel. You're gonna kill us!"

I began to wonder if this was all part of a cruel conspiracy to rid the world of me. Maybe my mother had planned this. That didn't seem likely. She loved me. Other than a wildly aggressive cowlick on the crown of my head, I was as close to perfect as a hyperactive kid could get. Then I remembered the number of times my mother had messed up the directions for Kraft macaroni and cheese, and I decided that she couldn't have planned this.

Perhaps Pastor Nolan masterminded this. Maybe he's not so interested in testing my faith, and instead he's trying to scare me into submission. But I didn't think that was possible either. He was originally from Georgia, and my father always told me that people from Georgia weren't too bright. He mentioned Jimmy Carter as an example.

When I could read the words on the sign we were about to run into, I grabbed hold of the armrest, clinched my butt cheeks together, and began doing breathing exercises in preparation for my near-death experience. As I inhaled through my nose and exhaled through my mouth, it suddenly occurred to me that people who encounter close calls with death often end up appearing on *Good Morning America,* and that was mildly exciting.

I might get to meet Joan Lunden.

"I guess Jesus had other plans for me, Joan," I would say to her when she interviewed me in my hospital bed, and then I would chuckle. Not too much of a chuckle, just enough to let America know I wasn't one of those near-death prima donnas who really were psychics trying to get ahead. After hitting the talk-show circuit, I imagined writing in a book that during my near-death encounter, I actually went to heaven and played Frisbee with Jesus and his dog, Steve.

We were about to run right smack into a sign advertising Maryland's new safety-belt campaign when I closed my eyes and dreamed of my moment in the spotlight with Joan Lunden. Three seconds later, I opened my eyes. We'd made it around the curve. Pastor Nolan was still looking in the rearview mirror, picking something out of his front teeth.

"You all right?" he asked.

"How did you do that?" I asked in amazement.

"How did I do what?"

"Steer the car without using your hands!"

"Oh, I've got very talented knees, Matthew. Haven't you heard anybody talk about my knees?"

"You steered the car with your knees?"

"Yep."

"Are you double jointed?" I asked.

"Nope."

"One of the kids at school is double jointed, and she can lick her own belly button."

"Lick her belly button?" he said. "Well, I can't do that, so I guess I'm not quite as talented as she is."

"You think it could have been angels?" I asked.

"No, just my knees. If it had been angels, I think I would have seen one or two fluttering around the car."

He drove the rest of the way to church using only his knees because he needed to finish getting ready. He dabbed on cologne. He pulled out an electric razor and shaved his five-o'clock shadow. Once when I blinked, I swear he crawled into the backseat and changed into pleated dress pants. In that moment, Pastor Nolan seemed more magical to me than Captain Kangaroo.

When we were about to pull into the parking lot of the church, he took hold of the steering wheel. "So, are you up for getting baptized next Sunday?" he asked.

I looked at him with hope in my eyes. "Will the water give me special powers?"

"Special powers? *No,* it won't give you any special powers. It's just something God commands you to do."

"I guess I'll get baptized. I want to make God happy."

"Terrific."

I watched as Pastor Nolan opened the car door, picked up his large black Bible, and tragically turned back into the man I feared, a preacher who, under most circumstances, wouldn't have been caught dead driving a car with his knees in front of a church kid. A man who wasn't allowed to be human.

Jesus in Black and White

My second-grade Sunday school teacher was a professional. Maybe not a big deal to some, but when I was seven, it made Patty Snover more interesting than all the other Sunday school teachers. Mrs. Snover kept her official Sunday school teacher certificate inside the front flap of her Bible. On Sunday mornings she would pull it out and tape it up on the classroom door, in case some smart aleck questioned her credentials. She'd point at it occasionally during her lesson, or while handing out candy, as a way of reminding us how far she'd come. It was encouraging that with a little faith, determination, and two hundred dollars for a weekend seminar in Indiana, we could go that far too.

My friend Callie seemed to be the perfect choice to follow in Mrs. Snover's footsteps. She was bigger than everybody else in the class, two years older, and rumored to have begun shaving her legs. Plus, she was one of the few students who believed that receiving a certificate of accomplishment was a big deal.

"Callie, you've memorized twenty-five Bible verses," Mrs. Snover said once. "Which means you get a gold certificate!"

Callie jumped out of her seat, cheered all the way down the aisle between our desks, and stood next to Mrs. Snover, bouncing like the next contestant on *The Price Is Right*. To this day, I am certain Callie thought she could trade that yellow paper in for a camper van and a seven-day, six-night Mediterranean cruise.

Earning her Sunday school teaching certificate really did make a difference in the way Mrs. Snover taught us Bible stories. Her first Sunday after the seminar, she taught on how the children of Israel made God angry and how he punished them by forcing them to wander in the wilderness for forty years.

"But God had a plan, boys and girls," Mrs. Snover said. "He wasn't going to let them starve out there, all alone. I bet the Israelites were like…"

She put her hands on her hips, cleared her throat, and said, "I'm just learning how to do this…," and then she began swinging her head from side to side. "But I bet God's people said something like, 'Whatchu talkin' 'bout, God? Wildaness? *Plan?* We needs a prospruss plan, God; dats all I gotts to say.'"

For a white woman's first attempt at speaking jive, it wasn't horrible. But her Harriet Tubman routine still seemed a little too Betty White.

"Anyway…it's something like that. I'll have to keep working on it," Mrs. Snover said. "But God did have a plan for the children of Israel. He wasn't just going to leave them stranded. God never leaves his people stranded."

Mrs. Snover told us to close our eyes.

"Children, I want you to imagine being in the wilderness with the Israelites."

Since I loved using my imagination, picturing myself in a wilderness was easy for me. I shut my eyes and thought about the one time my family drove through Ohio. As far as I knew, there was no place more wilderness-like than driving on Route 70 through the Buckeye State.

"Okay, kids, are you with the Israelites in the wilderness?" Mrs. Snover asked.

I wasn't exactly sure how to answer that. I was seventy-five miles east of Columbus, but I don't believe there was a Jew in sight. Lots of cows. But not one Jew.

"All right," she said. "*Now,* imagine how happy you'd be if you woke up in the wilderness to find God's little droppings all over the ground."

I heard something *plop* near my chair. Small objects were dropping all around me. A couple hit my table, and then one hit my face. Truly I was thankful that God was concerned about my well-being, but so far, the droppings weren't making Ohio much better.

"Keep your eyes closed! The Bible calls these droppings from God 'manna.' Who in this room wants to eat some of

God's heavenly droppings?" I heard Mrs. Snover move across the room. "You can now open your eyes."

When we opened our eyes, there were big marshmallows all around us.

"Feast on the droppings of God, children." Mrs. Snover clapped her hands, delighted. "Feast on his manna like there's no tomorrow."

I dropped to my hands and knees and crawled around the floor and collected as many of God's sugary droppings as I could, and I thanked him because he had given me bigger pockets than all but two other kids in my class.

Mrs. Snover was really quite creative when it came to illustrations. She made it very easy to believe that she knew everything there was to know about God.

One Sunday, Mrs. Snover handed each of us a black-and-white picture of Jesus grinning from ear to ear and holding two fish and five loaves of bread. She had just finished telling us how Jesus performed a miracle and fed five thousand hungry male followers. I'd heard that story many times before, but when Mrs. Snover pulled out a loaf of Wonder Bread and a couple of cans of Bumble Bee tuna to help us visualize the miracle, it opened my eyes to a new facet of that biblical story. Sometimes Jesus smelled like cat food.

As soon as Mrs. Snover handed me the coloring picture, I immediately jumped up and ran to grab the kelly-green and tangerine-orange crayons out of the coloring box. I began filling in Jesus's robe with my favorite shade of green.

"Matthew." Mrs. Snover darted around the table to where I was sitting. "What are you doing?"

"I'm coloring Jesus."

She didn't say anything at first; she just stood, rooted, and stared over my shoulder like a very disappointed nun. "Uh, no, no, no. Jesus's robe was not green, Matthew; it was white."

"Oh, this is not green." I held the crayon up and thrust it between her eyes. "It's *kelly* green." I was just about to explain to her the difference between kelly green and ordinary green, but she didn't give me a chance. Before I could say anything, Mrs. Snover's right eyebrow started twitching, and then her pudgy face wrinkled into a scowl. I sank back into my chair and concentrated on holding back tears. I knew that Mrs. Snover was the type of Christian woman who'd deemed it disrespectful to receive correction from any kid under the age of thirty-seven, no matter how politely put.

"It's still green, Matthew." Mrs. Snover's nostrils flared as she looked around at the white papers on the desks of the other kids. "Jesus didn't dress in those kinds of colors. He wore just a plain white robe."

Since I was only a second grader, I wasn't sure how she knew so much about the dress code of Jesus, but as I got older, I sometimes wondered whether or not she had been around him in one of her other lives, perhaps as one of the demons he cast out.

"I'm coloring Jesus the same colors as Aquaman," I said, looking down at my paper. It made perfect sense for Jesus to look like Aquaman. Not only was he holding a bunch of fish in this particular picture, but the week before, Mrs. Snover told us about Jesus's miracle of making a large school of fish jump into a net and sacrifice themselves so he could look good for his disciples. I was pretty sure his miracles didn't happen telepathically, but he certainly used some kind of super-hero strength to make those fish obey him.

"Well, I guess you have no choice but to continue coloring his robe green," said Mrs. Snover disappointedly. "Just make sure you leave his face white, okay?"

"I was going to." Everybody in the class knew Jesus was white.

"Well, at least your picture will be somewhat accurate," Mrs. Snover said.

I smiled.

"If you want to, we could call him Aqua Jesus."

She never did. Sometimes I wondered whether Jesus himself could have changed her mind.

I've often thought that it would have been nice having Jesus come to our Sunday school, where he could have explained some of the things we didn't understand. The kids in my class had lots of questions. Were we really his sheep? My father always said that sheep were the dumbest creatures alive.

"Nothing more stupid than a sheep," he'd tell me whenever we saw a flock fenced up along the side of the road. Did Jesus think we were stupid? Did he mean to insult us and comfort us at the same time? Or were we supposed to view the whole sheep comparison figuratively? Mrs. Snover didn't seem to think so. She'd sometimes pray and ask God to protect all the lambs in her class. "Shear them, Father," she'd pray. "Shear every one of them. And may their wool keep you warm and bring you glory. *Ahhhhman.*"

A part of me has always believed that God was bigger than how the people at my church talked about him. They thought of him as big, of course. And strong. One of the songs we used to sing in Sunday school boasted, "My God is so big, so strong and so mighty; there's nothing my God cannot do." We'd scream-sing those words so loud that our teachers would worry that our blood vessels would pop. But the big God that my pastor and Sunday school teachers talked about seemed like an if-he-ever-stepped-on-me-he'd-smash-me kind of big. Angry, giant big. It always made God seem unloving and uncoordinated.

The people at my church were always very certain of God. All of the most difficult questions about him seemed to be easily dispatched with a couple of Bible verses. "His ways are not our ways," was the standard answer for the unanswerable. Imagining God as anything less or more than how Pastor Nolan described him was a borderline abomination.

I suppose that's why a green and orange Jesus was ridiculous to Mrs. Snover. Coloring outside the lines was a chance no one was willing to take.

A few months later my mother and I were sitting on the

front porch. Mom was reading her Bible. I was eating my breakfast. I was notorious for asking random questions.

"Mom, does God wear clothes?" My mother stopped reading and looked up at me.

"Hmm, I don't really know. The Bible describes God as a spirit, but I'm not sure what that exactly means."

I took a sip of my orange juice. "So he might be up in heaven walking around naked?"

"I guess it's possible, I suppose. When he created Adam and Eve, they were naked in the Garden of Eden, but I don't really know if God wears clothes. I wish I did."

Over the years I've learned that sometimes God's mercy shows up in the form of a question, one that not only *can't* be answered, it was never meant to be.

You're a Big Boy Now

The kids in my church dreaded their twelfth birthdays, and with good reason. Pastor Nolan told us that God considered a kid of twelve old enough to know right from wrong. "And since you're old enough to be held accountable for your actions, God expects you to do what is *right*. Once you turn twelve, you can no longer use the excuse, 'I didn't know any better, Pastor Nolan.' *Why?* Because you're twelve and you *do* know better."

The church started holding us accountable for our actions on our twelfth birthdays—and that was the age we officially became eligible for hell. It wasn't exactly a bar mitzvah, but it was just as important. Eleven-year-olds had it made at our church. They could be skateboarding drug addicts who robbed grocery stores and killed bald eagles every other Tuesday and God would have still accepted them into heaven. But twelve-year-olds were toast.

"Let me put it this way." Pastor Nolan took a deep breath and massaged the back of his neck. "If you get into a car accident on your twelfth birthday and don't have Jesus in your heart, I think you'll go to hell. But if the car accident happened the day *before* your twelfth birthday, then I think you'll probably go to heaven. I don't think it's complicated. It's simple theology, people."

Even still, parents had many questions about this particular topic, questions Pastor Nolan didn't always know how to answer. They asked about the age of accountability for mentally handicapped people. They wanted to know what would happen if somebody went into a coma prior to turning twelve and never woke up. They inquired about whether or not this theory could be proven biblically and, if so, where in the Bible it could be found. Did the Bible contradict itself on the issue? And most of all, they wanted to know how Pastor Nolan came up with the magical age of twelve.

"Jesus was twelve when he went to the temple for the first time, so it seems to me that God thinks the age of twelve is pivotal for a young person."

I told myself I had nothing to worry about. For one thing, I'd invited Jesus to live inside my heart on many occasions, and secondly, by the time I was eight, I was spiritually astute for my size. While the other kids at church and school just seemed to get taller and fatter, I got holier.

If we had been part of the kind of religion that believed in reincarnation, bigger people might have wondered if I was

the apostle Paul or the prophet Daniel. I sometimes wondered this too. While I hadn't been struck blind on the road
to Damascus or slept with large, flesh-eating felines, I did see
John 3:16 pasted to a road sign once and large house cats
seemed to follow me around and enjoy licking my ankles.

But even those who had biblical blood running through
their veins struggled with sin from time to time.

I wrestled with staying awake during church on Sunday
and Wednesday evenings. I thought going to church when it
was dark outside was a waste of time. Four and a half minutes
into any nighttime sermon, my head started bobbing around
like a wobbly plate on top of an amateur clown's balancing
act. Eventually, my head plopped against whatever or whoever was closest, comfortable, and reasonably compliant. It
wasn't picky. Sometimes it was my father's shoulder or leg it
landed on; other times it was my mother's breast or arm. I
slept soundly until the pastor finished his sermon or until I
sensed one of my parents moving around in an effort to get
the use of their shoulder or bosom back.

While watching *The Phil Donahue Show* one afternoon, I
became convinced that my sleeping-in-church problem was
something I couldn't help—that it was caused by narcolepsy.
My sleeping disorder wasn't exactly like the people on Phil's
show. Their inability to stay awake happened at random
moments, like while they were driving or having sex. I seemed
to have the kind that only affected small children on Sunday
and Wednesday nights after the sermon began.

"Do you think that's what I have?" I asked my mother, who sat on the couch, painting her toenails.

"What?" my mother said. "I wasn't listening."

"Do you think I could be a narcoleper? Like these people." I pointed at the television.

"A narcoleper?" she said, bringing her right foot as close to her mouth as possible and blowing on the wet polish. "Do you mean a narcoleptic? No, that's not why you fall asleep during church, Matthew. Nice try, though. I'm pretty sure you could stay awake if you wanted to."

My mother always thought she was smarter than me. On any topic of conversation, Mom always had a logical explanation.

"That's not true." I spun the recliner around to face her. "I can't help if I have a *disease* that makes me fall asleep during church. It's not my fault. God made me that way."

My mother laughed, admiring her toes. "Oh, Matthew. You crack me up, sweetie." She stood and walked to the kitchen. "A narcoleper!" She squealed and laughed again.

The next day I started telling the kids at school that I had narcolepsy. And many of them were impressed. One friend even told me she would pray for my healing.

Since I'd get no help from my family with my disorder, I tried to think of ideas to help me stay awake. Sometimes I wrote in the air with my finger during the pastor's sermon. By the time he got to his second point, the atmosphere around me looked like an overused chalkboard. Mostly I practiced

writing my name or drew trees or ducks. Sometimes I practiced over and over again my favorite letter to write in cursive:
D. If I wasn't paying attention, I could write the cursive D one
hundred times for no reason at all and thoroughly enjoy every
pencil stroke. I'd always wanted my name to begin with the
letter D, something like David or Daniel or even Damien or
Dartmouth, so I could have written it more often.

When writing became dull, I organized the contents of
my mother's purse, a task akin to introducing fidelity to *The
Love Boat*. I enjoyed it, though, because I learned a lot about
my mother that way. How we were alike, how we were different. Neither of us minded hard candy being a little stale.
But she preferred spearmint, and I liked wintergreen.

My mother's pocketbook had lots of zippered slots. As I
scoured through each compartment, I found small wads of
cash tucked away in different places. I think keeping her
money in varied locations made her feel safer, but sometimes
she forgot where she put it. Weeks or months later, when she
found a five or twenty inside one of the more inconspicuous
side-zipper compartments, it became a miraculous reason for
her to run to the mall and splurge on a new pair of shoes
while busting out a couple of stanzas of "Count Your Many
Blessings."

My mother also kept secrets tucked inside her purse. I was
the only one in the family who knew about her habit of col-
lecting ink pens. The bottom of her purse was like the top
drawer of a secretary's desk. She had more ink pens than any

one person could use in a lifetime. She didn't just collect the basic Bic ballpoints either—her fascination with ink-based writing utensils was exotic. There were gold ones, silver ones, fat ones, cushioned ones, ones that wrote in red and green, and erasable ones. I never told anybody about her ink addiction. She and I had a silent agreement. If I didn't mention the pens, she wouldn't talk about my odd habit of reading the manufacturing comments on the back of toiletries like makeup compacts, Chap Stick, tubes of toothpaste, and bottles of shampoo or conditioner. I learned a lot of interesting information reading product packaging. I couldn't tell you what hymn we sang or how well the church soloist hit her high note, but at a very early age I knew how to properly lather, rinse, and repeat.

But not even the ingredients in my mother's travel-sized hairspray kept me from passing out on the pew.

Unfortunately, I never convinced my mother and father that my habit of taking naps during church was caused by a rare medical condition, one I was certain could be cured with medication, several dips in the Jordan River, or by putting my palm against the television whenever Pat Robertson was on. My parents believed my church drowsiness wasn't a sign of ill health but rather a spiritual disorder caused by my sinful disinterest in biblical-based preaching and that my condition was easily treatable with a little prescribed self-discipline.

"Matthew, I need to talk to you about something." My father didn't give lectures often, but I knew one was coming when he spoke to me the same way Papa Smurf spoke when bestowing wisdom upon his Smurflings. I wouldn't have admitted this to him, but when I was little, my father sometimes reminded me of Papa Smurf. He didn't have a bushy white beard, he wasn't bite-sized, and he thought any man who wore red pants was a communist, but like Papa Smurf's, Dad's tone made him seem five hundred years old. I found a strange comfort in that. His wisdom was like one of the antiques my grandmother kept on the mantle, high above her fireplace and out of my reach. It was precious and valuable, something I couldn't hold in my hands, which made me want to all the more.

"Your birthday is coming up in a few days," said Dad, sitting next to me on the porch swing. "How old are you going to be again?"

"Nine," I said. "Nine years old, Dad."

I said it twice because his question wasn't rhetorical, nor was he trying to be funny. He really didn't know. Dad forgot things like my sisters' and my exact ages, the dates of our birthdays, and where he'd put our Social Security cards. Usually his guess was close, but it had a margin of error of plus or minus two years.

"You're growing up, aren't you, son?"

I nodded, nervously awaiting how the next ten minutes would change my life.

"Well, son." Dad rubbed his hands together slowly, as if he'd dabbed on too much Vaseline Intensive Care. "Your mother and I have been talking about a few things."

The conversation began to scare me. Dad seemed to be

choosing his words carefully—not in an anxious way, but like he was on a mission from God, or Mom, or some semi-omnipotent combination of the two.

"Actually, we've been discussing some things about you." Dad cleared his throat. "And son, we've decided you're old enough to stay awake during the church service." He stopped rubbing his hands and began scratching the top of his head. "That means no more sleeping during the preacher's sermon. You're a big boy." He stopped scratching and looked at me. "You understand?"

"But—"

That was the only word I got to say in the entire conversation.

"No buts, son." Dad's voice became sterner. "From now on, we want you to stay awake and pay attention to the sermon. That's the way it's going to be."

I knew better than to say "but" again. Instead, I thought about all the buts I would have said if I'd been allowed to speak.

How was I going to stay awake and pay attention to the pastor's sermons?

How could I help getting tired?

Had Dad forgotten about my inability to pay attention to anything more than six minutes long? Unless it was animated, and even then, there were stipulations. For instance, I'd decided that Japanese animation gave me hives, so I had sworn off Speed Racer for life.

"So, are we clear on this, Buck?" asked Dad.

"I think so," I said, still wishing I could insert one more but.

I respected my father too much to tell him that this particular wisdom of his worried me. I worried because I'd always known my father to be the only member of my family with any true grasp on reality. From time to time, that reality spurred him on to refer to the Easter bunny as Satan's plush toy, but still, Dad had a lot of common sense. And even though I was young, I knew common sense was sometimes a fundamentalist's only saving grace.

Staying awake in church proved to be challenging for me. It wasn't keeping my eyes open that gave me trouble. That ended up being pretty easy. Every time my eyelids tried to close, I rubbed spit on them. If that didn't work, my father's hand could reach the entire length of the pew and find a way to inspire them open. Dad wanted me to listen to the sermon. Mom wanted me to take notes. Eventually, I needed no inspiration.

As it turned out, Pastor Nolan was wrong about the age at which a kid becomes accountable. I was nine when it happened to me. It didn't seem to matter to my parents that Pastor Nolan said Jesus was twelve when God started holding him accountable. I figured that was because Jesus wasn't a fundamentalist. I was the one becoming a fundamentalist— old enough to receive eternal punishment but too young to drink Mountain Dew.

To Hell and Back

I never met my great-uncle Leon. I wish I had. Many years before I was born, he married a fifth wife and moved to Idaho. He was my paternal grandfather's youngest brother, the rowdy black sheep of the family with big taste buds for trouble and mischief. The stories my father told about Uncle Leon made him seem larger than life, but in a worthless kind of way. I imagined him being Pecos Bill with cold sores.

My father was a lively storyteller. And whenever he told a story about Uncle Leon, he became especially animated.

"Uncle Leon got out of the car," my father explained. "Your granddaddy—*my father*—could already tell there was something wrong. As soon as he saw ol' Leon walking toward us, he looked at me and said, 'Boy, your uncle's looking shaky again.' Then he scratched the side of his head and mumbled, 'I wonder what he's gotten himself into this time.'

"Then," my father continued, "just about the time your

granddaddy was going to inquire about his behavior, Uncle Leon blurted out, 'Virgil…'"

My father looked at me and asked, "You know your granddaddy and I had the same name, right?"

I nodded.

No matter how many times I nodded throughout my childhood, every time he referred to his father's first name, he asked me that same question again.

"Anyway," Dad said, "Uncle Leon looked at my daddy and said, 'Virgil, I did something really stupid. I went to see a fortune-teller!' Oh, Matthew, I wish you could have seen your granddaddy's eyes. They got as wide as cow patties! He jutted out his bottom lip about a foot from the rest of his face and started yelling. 'A FORTUNE-TELLER? Do you got any brains in that head of yours, Leon?'"

Dad looked at me.

"Buck, you've heard me say this before, but your granddaddy cussed like a sailor. And he started cussing Uncle Leon up one side and down the other. Finally, he stopped and asked, 'Where in land's hill did you find a fortune-teller in these parts?'

"Uncle Leon's face got red as a Santa suit, and that's when he looked at the ground and said, 'It was a gypsy fortune-teller.'

"Oh boy, that made your granddaddy even angrier! He took off his hat and threw it down and yelled, 'You been messin' around with gypsies?' Matthew, your granddaddy didn't like gypsies. He thought they were good for nothin' except stealing and being lazy. He looked at Uncle Leon and asked, 'Where'd you find these gypsies?'

"Uncle Leon said to him, 'There's a band of gypsies camping out on a farm a few miles from here.' Then your granddaddy told him, 'You've really done it this time, Leon!' Your granddaddy paced the driveway, shaking his head and stomping his feet. And that's when he said, 'I have a great mind to take this here crowbar and bop it upside your head! Maybe it would rattle something loose up there, boy! You know better than to mess with them gypsies! You ain't got sense enough to come in out of the rain sometimes.'

"Then Uncle Leon said, 'I haven't even told you the worst part, Virgil. The fortune-teller read my palm and told me my future wasn't looking so good. She's got me so scared I can hardly think straight.'"

This is how Uncle Leon, who I never met, played an influential role in my life. When I was in third grade, an unexpected thing happened: Uncle Leon died and went to hell. That's what happened. He was at his home in Idaho, recovering from a serious surgery. His fifth wife was in the room next to his when she heard Uncle Leon scream like a doomed teen in a horror film. When she ran into his room, she yelled, "Leon, what's the matter?"

As soon as the question dropped out of her mouth, he sat up in bed, looked at her, and said, "I see hell."

And then he died.

. . .

When I was a kid, I needed hell to exist. I didn't understand that at the time, but I needed it. Being a fundamentalist was pointless without hell. With no hot and fiery pit existing somewhere below the soil, our views and beliefs lost a good deal of their meaning. It was our fear of hell that fueled our motivation for living the way we did. Perfect. Separated. *Medieval.*

What's strange is that *how we lived* didn't save us from eternal destruction. That only happened by being born again in the blood of Jesus. But being perfect, separated, and *content* with living in the Dark Ages helped us *feel* born again.

Feeling born again was much more difficult than actually *being* born again, but to us they seemed equally important. If we didn't feel saved, we had to get resaved. It got very complicated sometimes, but that's why hell was so important. It kept our minds in the game. Fear kept us faithful, like a rabbit scurrying in front of us and we were the greyhounds running as fast as we could to get to the finish line.

Believing in hell was just as important as believing in God. Sometimes more important.

My church celebrated the love of God, redemption through Jesus, and some of the gifts of the Holy Spirit. But all of that meant nothing unless 99 percent of the people living in China were going to burn in hell.

I couldn't help feeling sorry for Chinese kids. Finding

Jesus seemed more difficult for them. They didn't have churches on every corner. Preachers weren't allowed to have television shows. And Jesus never got advertised on billboards. An evangelist once came to IBBC and told us that Chinese people's only hope was if they happened to run into a Christian missionary, asked Jesus into their hearts, forsook their families, and went into hiding.

According to the missionary, that was the grace of God.

Hell was where the devil lived. Escaping the eternal torment in the next life meant you needed to escape the devil in this one.

I thought the devil was easy to spot when I was younger. To me, he stuck out like a black dot on a white sheet of paper. I'd be minding my own business and all of a sudden—*boo!*—Satan jumped out from behind a corner like he was a jack-in-the-box. He sought out ways to devour me, tempt me, or get me to take up smoking. I was trained in Sunday school to spot the devil. My teachers told me to watch out for roaring lions, disgruntled angels, women wearing low-cut blouses, and Billy Graham. Those were sure signs that Satan could be close.

But our Sunday school teachers also equipped us to defeat the devil.

"Kids, if you see the devil coming around the corner, what should you do?" asked Mrs. Snover.

"Tell him to go sit on a tack!" I screamed, since one of the songs we sang said that was a good idea.

"No," she said. "Anybody else?"

"Run," another child yelled.

"Yep, run like Carl Lewis ran in the 1984 Olympics," said Mrs. Snover. "Like the wind."

But running didn't always work. When I was five, I had a recurring dream that Satan lived in my grandfather's tool shed. In my dream, my sister Elisabeth and I were playing in the empty lot just over the hill from my grandparents' house. On the walk back, we had no choice but to pass right by the shed. Though we tried to sneak past, Satan always saw us and chased us with a screwdriver in his hand. We ran as fast as we could, but we were never fast enough.

Pastor Nolan told us that sometimes running from Satan wasn't an option. "Sometimes, people, you have to turn and fight against the strength of the devil."

Once a year, at his annual boxing match with Satan, he showcased the surefire way to defeat the agile boxing skills of the evil one. The three Sundays leading up to the night on which Pastor Nolan would duke it out against the Prince of Darkness, the devil came to our auditorium and interrupted the announcements.

"Hello, Preacher, it's me again!" Satan mocked. He spoke with the eloquence of a born-again redneck. "One of my demons tells me there's a man of God in this building. You wouldn't know who that is, would you?"

It felt weird standing on my pew and booing Satan at the top of my lungs. But since everybody else did the same thing, it was also weird not to.

"I'm the man of God around these parts." Pastor Nolan gripped his belt with one hand, smacked his Bible against the pulpit with the other, and swaggered up to the front of the stage. "What business does the devil have in *my* church? You here to get saved?"

"Uh, no."

"Baptized?"

"Not a fan of water."

"Then what brings you here, *devil?*"

"Well, I've been out partying with friends, drinking beer, and neckin' with some hot babes—the unchristian kind. But then it dawned on me that I was supposed to come to Chestertown and beat up on a man of God."

Having the devil in our church was always exciting—even if he was just one of the deacons or ushers dressed in a red leotard, black shorts, and a red mask with horns. For some of the deacons, the look fit.

Besides, when the devil came to visit, it made the service go faster.

The men dressed as Satan incarnate always portrayed him as a raging alcoholic. Satan would stumble up the church aisle with a bag-covered bottle in his hand. The bottle was important. It was usually just an old Coke or Tab bottle, but it deterred anybody from thinking Satan's drunkenness was the doing of the Holy Spirit. The mask scared me, partly because I wondered if they ever washed it, but it was also very ugly. Despite my church believing that Lucifer was one of God's most beautiful creations, according to Scripture, an *ugly* Satan seemed most practical, since nobody wanted any of the smaller children to develop a phobia of angels.

"Well, I hate to tell you this, Satan, but you've arrived four weeks too early. Our boxing match is scheduled for one month from today."

"I'll put that on my calendar, Mr. Preacher. Prepare to meet your doom."

On the day of the big match, rather than his usual coat and tie, Pastor Nolan walked onstage wearing sweatpants and a "God Is on My Side" T-shirt. As loudly as we had booed the devil, we cheered more loudly for Pastor Nolan, God's Chosen Man.

As a kid, sometimes I fought off the temptations of the devil by throwing a couple of air punches at him. "Oh, no you don't, Satan," I would say aloud. "You are not going to trick me into sneaking a Fig Newton out of the kitchen cabinet without asking."

If mere words didn't curb my urge for bite-sized portions of fruit and cake, I'd throw a left punch, then a right, and finish with an uppercut right to Satan's jaw. "Do not mess with me, Satan. You don't want me to start quoting the fifty-eight verses of Scripture I've got memorized."

That was how Pastor Nolan eventually won the boxing

match. After getting beaten to a pulp in the first two rounds—having purposefully leaned on his *own* understanding and strength and not God's—during the final round, he came out swinging his King James Version of the Bible like a sword and yelling the words of the apostle Paul. "'There is therefore now no condemnation to them which are in Christ Jesus,' Satan," he hollered.

He was right too. At least, when it came to boxing matches, since condemnation never once fell on Pastor Nolan. Nothing brought the devil to his knees like the words of the King James Version of the Bible. The old English verbs seemed to bruise Satan's skin more than the ones we used in normal conversation. Within seconds of hearing a "thou" or a "thy," Satan fell like a brick.

Knockout. Pastor Nolan 1, Satan 0.

This might seem odd, but hell was a hobby to some of the folks in my church. On Tuesday evenings, the church held gatherings for artists who enjoyed painting ceramics, mothers who wanted to learn how to raise godly children, and theologians who enjoyed debating which of the three layers of hell Geraldine Ferraro would end up in when she died.

One of those theologians was a deacon named Stanley. In case he happened to meet somebody who believed hell was a figment of their imagination, Stanley carried a handmade brochure about hell in his back pocket as well as a packet of matches. At our church, Stanley was the resident expert on all things biblically tormenting. If you wanted to know what the Bible said about famine, drought, earthquakes, or jock itch, Stanley was your go-to guy. He knew as much about human pestilence as Moses, and just like Moses, he seemed fully capable of bringing it to pass.

"There's going to be another flood," he said to my Sunday school class once. Stanley widened his eyes and pointed at my classmates and me. "It's going to make the last flood look like a walk in the park! Boys and girls, I think the Bible is pretty darn clear that this one is going to be a nuclear flood."

I made a mental note to talk to my father about building us a bomb shelter, preferably one with cable television. Stanley blamed the end of the world on MTV, and I wanted to see if the rumor about Kurt Loder becoming the antichrist would come true.

"According to my calculations," Stanley told us, "God's already secured Russia's involvement in this flood, and you can expect East Germany to be involved too! And believe me kids, there won't be any pretty rainbows at the end of this one. It's going to be a catastrophe. A catastrophe!"

Stanley was one of two people disappointed when the Berlin Wall crumbled. Mr. Gorbachev was the other. It makes sense Stanley would be saddened by the fall of the iron curtain, because speculating on the destruction of humankind didn't have the same buzz factor without communism. Its downfall made the possibility of his predictions coming true a lot less probable. And I suppose that wasn't nearly as much fun.

On several occasions I witnessed Stanley talking to people about hell. He talked about it the same way other people talked about traffic or the weather. "Oh, it's a mess down there," he would say. "I wouldn't be caught dead there." When Stanley met people who didn't believe there was such a place, he pulled out his brochure and showed them the proof he'd created and photocopied as handouts.

"It's as real as the building you're standing in," he said upon meeting someone who didn't believe in hell. "See? Here are some pictures. Now, these are only one artist's drawings"—Stanley looked seriously at the individual—"but I can assure you that everything you see depicted in them is biblically accurate. See? There's the devil."

At my church, biblical accuracy made pictures depicting the gnashing of teeth seem more like a work of art.

One of Stanley's protégés became my third-grade Sunday school teacher. Moose Casey looked like a normal man from the neck down. He had an average build that I only saw dressed in a three-piece pinstriped suit of wool or polyester. Since it resembled that of a spider monkey, it was Moose's face that kept people's attention. His eyes bulged slightly out of their sockets. His nose and mouth were smashed into each other like they had been installed as a single unit. And his beard was often unkempt looking, which made it the perfect habitat for something with a thorax.

One week, Moose walked into Sunday school carrying a paper bag from Dollar General. He ducked behind his pulpit and stuffed the paper bag inside one of its compartments. Moose's pulpit wasn't extravagant. Like most of the pulpits at our church, it was made of solid oak, painted white, and the same size as a duplex in Wisconsin.

When it was time for Moose to deliver that morning's sermon, he stood like a soldier behind his pulpit. He wore an interesting grin. It was the kind of expression one expected from a magician with a fancy rabbit trick or from Kathie Lee Gifford. Whatever he had up his sleeve, Moose seemed far too prepared for his own good.

"This morning's talk begins with a question," Moose said. "It's an important question, so listen carefully, boys and girls."

It was odd that Moose had decided to announce that his sermon began with a question, because all of Moose's Sunday school sermons began with questions. Questions that bordered on ridiculous. Questions he screamed at us at the top of his lungs. The question from the week before had been, "WHO'S YOUR WORST ENEMY?"

Whenever Moose screamed at us, the veins on his forehead became engorged until they were bigger than sausage links. That frightened me. Since I sat in the second row, I worried his head might explode and make a mess on my Sunday clothes.

"WHO'S YOUR WORST ENEMY?" Moose screeched a second time. "DOES ANYBODY HERE KNOW?"

Of course, we knew who our worst enemy was. We were Baptists, not Lutherans. That information had been indoctrinated into us as fetuses. Most of us came out of the birth canal already feeling passive-aggressive toward Satan. So I raised my hand and announced that Satan was our worst enemy. I said it with great assurance.

But I was wrong.

Satan wasn't our worst enemy. Not according to Moose. That didn't stop six other kids from shooting up their hands and offering other surnames of the Prince of Darkness. As young Baptists, we were well versed on Lucifer's many monikers. Most of us had taken a church-sponsored devil's workshop on all things Angel of Darkness. We learned that Abaddon was the Prince of the Air, which meant he liked rock radio and, on occasion, Barry Manilow. Beelzebub enjoyed infiltrating children's programming, as we learned that Azrael, the cat from *The Smurfs*, was actually the Great Tempter drawn in cute kitty animation. Since we knew so much about Satan, it made no sense to us why he wasn't our biggest enemy.

But still, I had answers. "Madonna," I shouted. "Madonna is our worst enemy. She makes fun of the Virgin Mary."

"No!" Moose yelled.

"How about Michael Jackson?"

"Nope."

Moose pulled out a hand-held mirror and panned it across the room so each of us could get a glimpse of our worst enemy.

"YOU ARE YOUR WORST ENEMY! YOU! YOU! YOU! YOU DECIDE WHETHER OR NOT YOU GO TO HELL! IT'S ALL UP TO YOU!"

That's when I began seeing a therapist.

On the morning of the paper bag, Moose's question was even odder. He looked at us and screamed, "BOYS AND GIRLS, DO YOU KNOW HOW HOT HELL IS?" He was serious, as if speaking to a room full of Christian meteorologists. "DOES ANYBODY HERE KNOW?"

As soon as Moose asked the question, I looked at my friend Angie. If anybody in our Sunday school class had visited hell and remembered to take a thermometer, it would be her. Not only was Angie always well prepared and organized, but she also claimed to make frequent visits to far off places when she slept. One time, during a nap, we heard her mumbling in tongues. When she woke up, she told us she had taken a vacation to Montreal and been able to speak French. When she saw me looking at her, she raised her hand.

"Mr. Moose, the temperature of hell is 666 degrees," said Angie with the enthusiastic confidence of a demon. "Everybody knows that! Or should."

I thought her answer was brilliant—possibly even correct—despite the fact I never believed she'd gone to Montreal.

Moose grew quiet. He didn't tell Angie she was wrong, but he didn't tell her she was right either. He just walked over to the door and shut off the lights. Moose's Sunday school helper, Penny, placed large sheets of fabric underneath both of the doors to block the light coming in. The room became almost black. Moose stood behind his pulpit and found his Dollar General bag.

"This morning, I want to talk to you about hell." His voice was quiet and low. He wanted it to sound spooky, and it did. "What's hell like? It's black down there. Much blacker than what you're experiencing right now. Imagine a black so thick you can almost feel it. That's what hell is like."

I heard Moose rummaging through his paper sack and then the distinct sound of a Play button being pushed on a tape recorder. The crackling noise of the tape began. And then voices.

"It's hot down here!" said the tape recorder. "We are thirsty! Very thirsty. We need Jesus."

"Do you hear that, boys and girls?" asked Moose. "That's what you would hear in hell. There would be a lot more of them, though. And some of the voices you wouldn't be able to understand because they're from other countries."

While I assumed Moose was right, that his tape of sound effects could have been a live audio recording of hell, I was also convinced that if I closed my eyes during church fellowship time, when a long line of Christians waited for Ho Hos and fruit punch, it might have sounded similar.

Moose put his hand into the bag and pulled out something else. Penny turned on a flashlight and shined it toward the front of the room. Moose held what looked like a knockoff of Suntan Barbie. He held it up for all of us to see.

"Kids, meet Sally," Moose said. "Sally is pretty. She has a

great job. Her husband loves her dearly. Sally takes her two kids to church on Sunday morning. But do you want to know something very sad about Sally?"

A kid named Jeff shot up his hand. "I know why she's sad, Mr. Moose!" he said as fast as he could get the words out. Jeff was the most hyper kid in our class, but he was smart. He knew things most third graders wouldn't learn for another eight or nine years, if ever. The poor kid couldn't pay attention, but he didn't really need to. Most of the time he just stared at the floor, bounced on his seat, and calculated in his head how he would get to Neptune someday.

"It's because she's plastic!" said Jeff in a hurry. "That's right, isn't it? She's not a real girl! Like Pinocchio wasn't a real boy. Do you know some people think that *really* happened? That's insane, isn't it? You know another thing I learned, Mr. Moose—"

"That's a good thought," said Moose, interrupting Jeff and attempting to move on. "But no, the really sad part about Sally's life is that she has lung cancer."

Jeff shot up his hand again but didn't wait to be called on before he spoke. "She's plastic, Mr. Moose!" he said, putting both of his hands on his head and throwing his body back against the chair. And then, in a matter-of-fact manner, he asked, "How does a plastic doll get lung cancer? That's the craziest thing I've ever heard! It's preposterous. Next you'll tell me that G.I. Joe came home from Santa Monica with frostbite or something. It's *that* crazy!"

Though he was brilliant, Jeff was born without an imagination. That made church difficult for him sometimes. But to him, far worse than remaining quiet during a Sunday school lesson about Noah's ark was being made to watch *MacGyver*. To Jeff, MacGyver was the Antichrist.

"*She was a terrible smoker,* Jeff!" said Moose defensively, trying to legitimize Sally's story. "We're talking two packs a day. So just listen to the story, okay? Listen with your ears and not your mouth. Anyway, as I was saying, Sally's got lung cancer and there's a good chance she's going to die. But the saddest part of Sally's story isn't her cancer, boys and girls; it's that she never asked Jesus into her heart. She's not a *Christian*! So, kids, where would Sally go if she were to die?"

"HELL!" we screamed enthusiastically.

"WHERE WOULD SHE GO?" yelled Moose.

"HELL!"

"AND DO YOU WANT TO GO TO HELL, BOYS AND GIRLS?"

"NO!" we screamed.

"That's right!" Moose held Sally up high. "I don't want to see this happen to any of you."

Moose reached into his pocket, pulled out an orange cigarette lighter, and flicked on the flame. As he held Sally by her lustrous blonde hair, he put the small flame just under her rubbery feet. "THIS IS WHAT HAPPENS IN HELL, BOYS AND GIRLS!" he screamed. Then he set Sally's feet on fire.

"SEE WHAT HAPPENS TO HEATHENS THAT SMOKE?" yelled Moose, and he began to cough. As Sally's body turned into toxic fumes that made their way to each of our lungs, our classroom began to sound like an infirmary where every patient had a smoker's cough. It occurred to me that this might be what hell *really* sounded like.

"SOMEBODY OPEN THE DOORS!" cried Moose. "SEE? THIS ONLY PROVES YOU DON'T WANT TO GO TO HELL!"

Cough. Cough. Cough.

"Whoever wants to ask Jesus into your heart, raise your hand, and then follow me."

Cough.

That was the fourth time I asked Jesus into my heart, and the third time I got baptized. I figured that, even if Jesus was in my heart prior to Moose's Barbie-burning fiasco, there might have been a chance the fumes I inhaled ran him off. So I invited him again.

I didn't want to end up like Great-Uncle Leon.

I needed hell to exist. It helped me focus. It kept me striving toward being a good fundamentalist. It caused me to pray and read my Bible. It even helped me turn off the television when T. J. Hooker said a bad word.

I wouldn't have been a Christian without hell. I guess it's kind of like sex—it sells.

You Know Where Liars Go

learned what it felt like to hate somebody in the fourth grade. That's the year Pastor Nolan's mother moved to Chestertown from Georgia and became my teacher.

I went to a Christian school. You weren't considered a good independent fundamental Baptist unless you attended an independent fundamental Baptist school. Period. So when I was in first grade, my parents enrolled me in Bible Baptist Christian School. When Mom and Dad told me that I would be going to a new school, I walked into my kindergarten class at Worton Elementary the following day and announced to my class that I would not be coming back next year. Mrs. Hessey gave me a perplexing look and said, "That makes me sad, Matthew. Why won't you be coming back?"

"Because my church believes public schools are for heathens," I told her. I think she understood, because after that, she didn't ask me any more questions.

The Baptist school "rule book" warned parents in the opening letter from the principal that our school offered a kindergarten-through-twelfth-grade, God-centered education. In the beginning, Pastor Nolan created my school to be a way for parents who attended IBBC to protect and separate their children from the world. Eventually though, unable to financially support itself, the school opened its doors to students of other Christian denominations—not including Catholics—as long as the students and their parents signed a contract stating they had been born again in the blood of Jesus and would live their lives according to the school's rule book.

Some people considered the school a godsend, a way to protect their children's precious minds from hearing, learning, reading, or believing in things like evolution, secular philosophies, or the 1984 platform of the Democratic Party. Others called my school God's little boot camp.

For me, the school personified the church. At church, Pastor Nolan taught us *how* to be a fundamentalist, but it was at school that his teachings became a way of life enforced by the teachers.

So, yeah—a boot camp.

From spelling to algebra, Jesus was infused into every aspect of our education. Our science books didn't simply teach intelligent design. That would have been blasphemous. Our textbooks told us the world had been Jesus-designed in exactly six twenty-four-hour days. I learned that the dinosaurs no longer existed because Noah couldn't fit them on the ark.

George Washington, Thomas Jefferson, and Benjamin Franklin were born-again Christians and not only believed that the United States of America was a *Christian* nation but also considered America to be God's "new Israel."

No other teacher was better at enforcing the rules than Nanny Nolan. She was somewhere between 60 and 274 years old but didn't look a day over 73. On the day I met her, I told my father, "This isn't going to be a good year."

"Ah, Buck, don't say that," Dad said. "It'll be great."

I didn't believe him. By then I'd learned that, in regard to our school, my father's optimism was actually just good-natured denial.

"You need to have a good attitude, son."

I nodded. "I know."

It was Tuesday, and Mrs. Nolan came to class wearing the outfit she normally wore on Thursdays. She seemed very fond of how she looked in that particular dress. I once overheard her telling her teaching assistant, Mrs. Bark, that she believed the pink and white corduroy jumper made her look thinner. It didn't. It made her look like a bottle of Pepto-Bismol.

But I knew better than to tell her that. Instead, I smiled at her when I walked into class and said, "Hello, Mrs. Nolan. You look so pretty today. I love that pink dress." I sat my bookbag next to my chair. "There aren't many women who could pull off that outfit."

That I believed, but it wasn't because Mrs. Nolan was

doing the outfit any favors. No other woman should ever attempt to pull off that dress. Or put it on, for that matter.

"Thank you," said Mrs. Nolan in a tone that made it obvious she didn't believe me.

At some point during the semester I'd gotten into the habit of paying Mrs. Nolan random compliments three or four times a day. I felt obligated because she didn't like me and I wanted her to. She was an authority figure in my life, and I needed her to like me, so I did my best to earn her acceptance.

Prior to meeting Mrs. Nolan, I'd never been disliked by anyone before, especially an older woman. Old women fell head over heels for me. I didn't even have to try—it just happened. I thought I had a gift. As soon as I walked into church, women over the age of thirty-four threw candy at my feet like I was Mick Jagger and the Tootsie Rolls were underwear. But Mrs. Nolan was indifferent to the charm other women saw in me. She wasn't impressed with me.

I really needed her to be impressed.

At my church and school, perception was everything. How people viewed you was much more important than how you actually were. The truth didn't matter. What people *believed* to be the truth mattered. I learned early on that if everybody believed I was the well-behaved, good-natured boy without a sin in the world, it didn't matter what the truth was. The truth was secondary to a person's opinion or perception of the truth. It was all about good PR, and prior to having Mrs. Nolan as a teacher, nobody stared at me too closely.

That was why each day I came up with something flattering to say to her. I hoped that one day I would find something that moved her to show some kind of affection. A smile. A pat on the back. A nonfrown would have been nice. Some days I came into school and complimented one of the dozen outfits I'd seen her wear over and over again. Other days I expressed how lovely her hair looked when she teased it out like a troll. During the Christmas season I even commended her handwriting. "I bet it's just as pretty as the Virgin Mary's," I told her as she wrote in cursive on the chalkboard.

My sister Kelley helped me brainstorm ideas. Though she was eight years older than me, Kelley and I were the middle children, and I think that helped us understand each other. "Have you complimented her teeth?" she asked as I sat on the bathroom vanity and watched her carefully apply blue eye shadow. "Most women really like to have people say nice things about their teeth."

She smiled into the mirror, checking to make sure her own teeth weren't showing any signs of breakfast.

"Really?" I said, mesmerized by Kelley's attention to detail, color, and volume of her eyelashes. "Even if they have dentures?"

"Absolutely. That might even be better." She pointed a tube of mascara at me. "If you compliment her dentures, she'll think you can't tell. Maybe you could tell her how white they are, or that they're nice and straight." She smiled into the mirror again, as if she'd forgotten how white and straight her own were. "I think that should make her feel really good about herself."

"But what if they aren't white and only sort of straight?" I asked. "Do I just lie?"

"Oh *please*, Matthew." She held a pair of tweezers between two fingers, preparing to pluck one of her eyebrows. "Last fall when you told her she had the nicest pumpkins of any teacher in the school, did you really believe that?"

"But at least her pumpkins were attractive," I said. "And I thought their stems were really nice. So it wasn't an all-out lie."

Kelley rolled her eyes. "You know Mrs. Jones's pumpkins are always the best. And what about all the times you've told her how much you love that hideous black dress she wears with the different colored squares all over it?"

"That dress isn't so bad," I said.

Kelley looked at me. "Not if you're a Rubik's Cube."

She was right. In addition to Mrs. Nolan looking like a Rubik's Cube in that dress—one tragically left unsolved—I was a liar. Almost instantly, my stomach began to ache with gas pains, which I always assumed meant the Holy Spirit was trying to tell me something. When Kelley left the bathroom, I stayed behind so I could spend time sitting on the toilet in prayer.

"I'm a liar, God," I said, reaching for the toilet paper. "I'm sorry."

Yep, you're a liar, the gurgle in my stomach said to me. *And I'll make you feel bad about it until you confess.*

I flushed the toilet.

■ ■ ■

A few months earlier, before corduroy was in season, Mrs. Nolan had stood at my desk, looking over a few sentences to which I had just finished adding commas. By the look on her face, I hadn't done such a good job.

To me, commas seemed like fickle creatures, and I never was very good at placing them where they were supposed to go. However, since Mrs. Nolan wasn't a real, certified teacher, she wasn't very good at placing them either. My school didn't require teachers to have college educations. Most of the teachers weren't professionals. At my school the kids taught themselves at their own pace using a curriculum that, in order to pass to the next grade, required twelve small booklets be completed in each subject. On that day Mrs. Nolan was checking my work to see if I was ready to take that book's exam. I started to get nervous because it was taking her so long.

"Are those new shoes, Mrs. Nolan?" I asked, looking down at a pair of tan loafers that looked like the kind that came with a prescription.

"No, they're not, Matthew." She pulled a green ink pen from the flap of her ear.

"Well, I really like them," I said. "They match your legs."

"Thank you, Matthew," she snapped. "They're comfortable."

For an old lady, Mrs. Nolan had excellent posture. She probably practiced standing perfectly straight in front of a mirror. She seemed like that kind of woman who worried about things like posture. She probably made her husband practice with her.

"Matthew!"

I looked up to see Mrs. Nolan's face crinkled like an angry raisin.

"What is this?" She pointed at a small red dot above one of the sentences. "Is that red ink? That's red ink, isn't it?" She turned a page. "And look, there's another!"

She was right—they were red ink dots. I put them there when I checked my own work at the checking table. And because I had been back and forth from my cell to the checking table about seven times, I eventually just put a couple of small, barely noticeable red dots above the spots where the commas belonged.

In other words, I cheated.

As soon as Mrs. Nolan began yelling at me, I didn't want to be there anymore. I wanted to go someplace else, someplace safer, someplace where angels played poker and didn't mind letting a cheater play along. I looked around my desk for anything that might make a suitable noose, but before I could prepare for my quick exit, the Holy Spirit showed up in my lower intestines and blew bubbles. I felt blood rushing from every part of my body and gathering like clots in my cheeks and forehead. A wave of nervous adrenaline washed over me as I tried as hard as I could not to look guilty.

But I was guilty. I felt guilty. And I was sure I looked guilty.

"I think you cheated," said Mrs. Nolan loudly. "You put those red dots there on purpose, so you wouldn't have to go back to the checking table. So you could come back to your seat and put commas there with your pencil. I'm right, aren't I?"

Don't look guilty, Matthew, I thought. *Don't look guilty.*

"No!" I said. "I can explain."

I was lying again. I couldn't explain. It hadn't crossed my mind that I needed to prepare an official statement or excuse to cover my tracks—or my red dots, as the case was. I wasn't a professional cheater, just one who dabbled in cheating from time to time, like somebody who sells Tupperware in the evenings for the free storage containers.

As Mrs. Nolan scanned my book for every red dot she could find, I did what I always did when I felt the pounding ache of anxiety and I couldn't find a guillotine: I prayed. *God,* I thought, *Do you help sinners? Do you even like sinners? If you do, please help me. P.S. You are awesome.*

Mrs. Nolan's voice filled the room in a tone I couldn't imagine Jesus ever using. "Oh, so you think you can explain, can you? I would love to hear your explanation, Matthew."

I thought about my mother and father and the pride and joy that would seep from their faces if they found out I had cheated. It was an unsettling experience to confess any kind of sin when you were a ten-year-old fundamental Baptist with a deacon for a father and a mother who thought the television should be taken outside and shot execution style. Confessing I was a cheater would have been like telling my parents I was Hindu and that I thought I was born that way.

I looked at Mrs. Nolan, and with the guilt of a thousand prisoners written across my face, I made up a very stupid lie.

"I must have accidentally hit the paper with the pen," I blurted. "When I was checking my work. The pen just hit the page a few times."

Once I said it out loud, it didn't sound nearly as stupid as it had in my head.

"Oh really?" said Mrs. Nolan. "And it just so happens that eight out of the ten marks are located where commas are supposed to go?"

It suddenly became stupid again.

I thought about suggesting that it might have been a miracle, but before I got the chance, her eyes got big, and an angry look appeared on her face. I thought she was going to do what the prophet Elijah did when a group of children mocked his bald head. I didn't know how a couple of grizzly bears would get into our classroom and eat me, but I was convinced that Mrs. Nolan did.

"That's it!" she yelled. "Go to the principal's office! I don't want your cheating soul in my class. I don't even want to look at you."

"But Mrs. Nolan—"

"Don't you say another word, Matthew Turner. Not another word. I feel sorry for you. You had your chance to confess your sins to me, and instead you lied. Everyone in this classroom heard you. God heard you. You lied! And you know it. Go."

I walked through the door and down the stairwell toward the principal's office. I felt alone and dirty and unprepared for what might come next. I'd never been *sent* to the principal's office before. I'd always gone there voluntarily for hall passes or to hand in a doctor's notice.

I thought about my friend Kathy. The week before, she had been caught cheating, and when she told the truth, she still got two days of suspension and a slew of dirty looks from Mrs. Nolan after she returned.

I thought about what my father might say. "You know where liars go, right, son?" He would then direct my attention toward the cat-o'-nine-tails he used to keep his pants from falling down.

When I opened the door to the principal's office, I felt like I was opening the gates of hell. The musty scent of wood paneling hit me in the face. I poked my head inside, and the secretary motioned for me to come in. It was obvious Mrs. Nolan had used the intercom to let her know why I was there. The secretary was a girl named Charlene, an older student who, on Tuesdays and Thursdays, filled in while the real secretary taught church aerobics to a group of women.

"The principal will be with you in a bit." Her face was pale and perfect like a china doll, and she had a comforting smile. She picked up a box of tissues and offered me one so I could wipe the tears and snot off my face. "It's going to be okay. You don't think it is right now, but it will be."

After only a couple of minutes, the door to the principal's office opened, and he ushered me inside. As he shut the door behind us, I caught a quick glimpse of Charlene. She winked at me like I imagined an angel doing. And she nodded her head as if to remind me again that it would be okay.

The following year a rumor spread around our school about Charlene. Some of the women in our church suspected she was sleeping with the principal. The truth never came out. Her parents pulled her out of the school, and I never saw her again. Sometimes I wonder if that's why she was so kind to me. Maybe she understood that, under our circumstances, the truth didn't always set you free.

Sometimes it just made you lie.

When I arrived at school the following day, the classroom seemed cooler. As soon as she saw me, Mrs. Nolan followed me to my desk, grabbed my arm, and turned me toward her. "You might have convinced the principal and your mother and father that you didn't cheat," she said, "but I know better, and I'm going to watch you like a hawk, young man!"

"Okay," I said and put my head down on my desk, begging God silently not to send me to hell. I told him I was sorry and pleaded with him to let Jesus come back into my heart.

Then I reached into my book bag and grabbed a container of Rolaids. Right before I popped one, I said, "Holy Spirit, forgive me."

Brought to You by the Letter *D*

When I was a kid, Jesus and I made a deal. Actually, I made the deal. Jesus just went along with whatever I said. He was very compliant. Much more than most Christians would ever admit.

The conditions of our agreement were simple: if I saved Jesus a seat on the school bus every morning, he would help me not to—as my mother put it—dillydally.

My dillydallying drove my mother crazy, and she made sure that I knew it. Every time she suspected it, she cleared her throat and said, "You're doing it again." She did that once while I innocently enjoyed the antics of a small insect crawling on the ceiling rather than write my spelling words five times each.

"What?" I said. "What am I doing?"

"Dillydallying!" My mother sat on the couch, looking at me with eyes that screamed, *"I don't want my only son to end up homeless or, God forbid, tempted to join the Peace Corps."*

My mother didn't get me sometimes. If she had, she would have realized how much it bewildered me that she only acknowledged the sins that I *did* do, never the ones I didn't. Just once I wanted her to look at me with an angelic smile and say, "Matthew Turner, you little dickens. I just have to say this: I am so proud of you."

Of course, I would shyly respond with, "*Me?*"—placing my hand across my chest—"You're proud of *me*? Really? What in the world for? I didn't do anything."

Then my mother could have said, even more brightly than before, "But that's just it, Matthew. My pride for you isn't because of something you did. I feel the need to affirm you for what you *don't* do, honey."

"*Really?* You want to stand up and give *me* a round of applause for what I *don't* do?" That's what I would ask her, and I would do it as if I'd never even pondered needing such an acknowledgment. "*Mom,* you don't have to do this. *Gosh.* You're far too good to me, you know that? Okay, go ahead and give it to me. What don't I do?"

It would have been easy.

She had a myriad of biblical sins she could point out as examples of what I *never* did. She could mention 95 percent of the sins listed in Deuteronomy.

I never coveted my neighbor's wife.

I never formed any graven images to worship.

I always hated crawfish.

And I would never have thought to let my herds dwell among the herds of those God hated.

But commending me for sins I avoided wasn't my mother's style. Maybe she thought the power of suggestion might cause me to ponder committing such sins, or maybe it just never crossed her mind that I might have enjoyed a celebration of the sins I easily abstained from.

Mom looked at me over the top of her reading glasses and said, "Matthew, you're still doing it."

I tried not to dillydally. I knew it was a sin. Pastor Nolan would have placed it under the sin of procrastination or the one about idle hands being the devil's workshop, or maybe he would have related it to Jesus's warning against tossing a good string of pearls to pigs. But whatever its category, I didn't know how to stop. Dillydallying happened without my realizing it. One minute I sat at the kitchen table, writing my spelling words like I was supposed to, and the next minute, I'd be in the middle of the kitchen floor, imagining I was a famous tap dancer on the verge of my first national title and about to offer a screaming crowd the gold-medal performance of a lifetime.

My mother had good reason to be concerned. I possibly should have been institutionalized.

"Matthew, here's the deal…"

With every bit of mental muscle I could muster, I turned my attention back toward the repetitious writing of my spelling words. But every word I wrote felt like one more clogged artery, slowly killing my soul. Being forced to sit and write my spelling words was like committing a very slow suicide. Besides, I didn't want to miss the bug trying to break dance on the ceiling.

"You probably think I sound like a broken record." I felt my mother's glare burning against the side of my skull. "But people who dillydally don't amount to much." My mother set her cup of coffee on the coffee table in front of her. "I'm pointing it out for your own good—because I love you. Because I want nothing but the best for you."

And then, as if trying to convince me her previous sentence was the honest-to-God truth, she added, "One of these days you'll thank me for how these conversations changed your life. You'll call me just to tell me that. You might even write me a letter or something. I know you don't think that's true right now, honey, but you will. And that day will feel like Christmas for me."

I wanted to look at my mother to portray that I was paying attention, but the events on the ceiling were much more interesting. The insect had bounced and buzzed its way from the corner of our living room to take a breather on one of the light fixtures. I was trying to figure out whether or not it was waving at me.

"Matthew?" My mother's voice got louder. "Matthew! You're not listening to me, are you? Look at me, son. *Sweetie.* Look at me. What in the world are you looking at?" She turned her head toward the ceiling, then back to me. Then back to the ceiling. "That bug? You're looking at that bug?" Her eyes got big. "Well, I can certainly take care of that, can't I?"

Before she finished her sentence, she came into the kitchen, staring me down with each step.

"What are you going to do?"

"I guess you'll have to pay attention to find out, won't you?" Mom seemed impressed with herself, having finally gotten my undivided attention. She grabbed a fly swatter from the top of the refrigerator and walked back into the living room.

"Don't hurt it!" I yelped. I waved my hands and prayed for God to intervene on behalf of that young bug's life.

The insect landed on the corner of the table my grandfather built. *Bam. Bam. Bam.* Just before the poor thing breathed its final breath, I watched it moonwalk.

"*Now,*" my mother said, picking up the bug's body with a tissue and heading toward the toilet, "you'll be able to concentrate on your spelling words."

I knew my mother's persistence wasn't about me finishing my spelling words. Like any mother, she wanted what was best for me, which meant she wanted me to become an independent fundamental Baptist preacher.

When she thought about my future, she saw visions of souls being saved, souls being baptized, and souls being bundled into sheaves—all because of my willingness to follow God into full-time ministry. She had the perfect scenario already worked out in her mind. I would graduate from high school, enroll in a good Bible college, marry an undefiled woman, and settle down as the pastor of a small church a fifteen-minute drive from wherever Mom would be living at the time.

That was God's ideal plan for me according to my mother.

"God has something very special for you, Matthew," she'd say with so much hope in her eyes. "I *know* that's true, and I don't want to see you waste it. Not on my watch."

Whenever Mom saw my young mind wandering aimlessly, she didn't view it as me simply wasting my own time. I was wasting hers too. I was wasting all the moments she'd spent on her knees asking God to make me into the man she so desperately wanted me to be. I was wasting all of the hours she had spent away from home, working at the mental hospital so she could afford to send me to a Christian school. I was wasting all the hopes and dreams she and my father hoped and dreamed for my future.

And that made her sad.

I never for a second believed that my mother enjoyed pointing out my mistakes. I think she hated it. There was a grief in her eyes whenever she was forced to remind me that I was human. My mother grieved because she was just like me—a dreamer with a nomadic soul who wouldn't mind having the freedom to be off course once in a while.

I don't think she resented getting married at eighteen, starting a family at twenty, and settling down in a small town with a degree in nursing. But sometimes, when I looked in her eyes, I could tell she felt stifled by life. And then she felt guilty for thinking that way. The truth is, my mother never felt comfortable being a full-fledged dreamer. She wanted to, but it was too unpredictable and often seemed wrong. I believe that was the reason she so easily became a fundamentalist. She wanted security and structure, and who better to organize her life than God?

For most of my life, I've watched my mother resist the urge to color outside the lines. Not because she didn't want to do it, but because some part of her wasn't free enough. On those occasions when she fought against my coloring outside the lines, it wasn't because she thought I shouldn't do it.

I think she tried to save me from feeling disappointment, or perhaps she feared that I wouldn't.

I made that deal with Jesus hoping he would help me concentrate on the things that truly mattered, or at least the ones that mattered to my mother. Even though I believed with all of my beating heart that Jesus and I were pals, BFFs, shared the kind of camaraderie some people don't believe exists, our friendship felt a little one-sided sometimes.

I can't remember ever failing to save Jesus a seat on the bus, which was much more difficult than it sounds. It was embarrassing when I had to look somebody in the eye and say, "I'm sorry. Jesus is sitting here," or "Can you please scoot over and make room for my Messiah?" But I did it because I enjoyed having him sit next to me. While some kids walked by the empty seat next to me with their noses in the air because I was about as cool as Jan from *The Brady Bunch*,

Jesus never did. Even though he was God's Son, the God-man who would someday be called King of kings and Lord of lords, he always had time to ride the bus with me.

But Jesus wasn't perfect. He struggled with his side of the bargain.

"Just help me remember," I prayed to him once. "Please. That's all I'm asking. If you notice me dillying or dallying, hit me or strike me with lightning or make a miraculous example out of me, but please, don't let me get away with it. Leave me a Post-it, even."

When my sixth-grade teacher, Mr. Kuntz, handed me my report card for the third quarter, I knew it wasn't going to be good. But I had no idea the signs of dilly and dally would be so obvious. Three Ds. I looked at my report card again and again, hoping I could will those Ds into Bs. Even Os would have been better than Ds.

Tears the size of melons rolled down both my cheeks as I imagined which decade my father would kick my backside into. One D wouldn't have been so bad. Two Ds would have gotten me grounded until the next report card, but I would have survived. But three Ds? That was an act of treason. My parents might divorce me or send me off to Paraguay or install a fiery furnace in my bedroom.

On the bus ride home, I didn't talk to Jesus. But not because I blamed him. I gave him the benefit of the doubt, which back then seemed to be what faith was in a nutshell. I was certain he had tried to help me, but because I was such a daydreaming sinner, I hadn't even noticed.

The whole ride home I stared straight ahead at the seat in front of me and pondered how I would tell my parents about my D-mented report card. *Hey, Mom and Dad,* I thought, *the good news is I got a* B *in gym, and the bad news is, um...* That wouldn't work. Who in their right mind considered a B in gym good news? I thought about starting with something about God, something to manipulate their spirituality. A few words about God's mercy might work, I thought. Maybe I could bring up the story of David hooking up with Bathsheba and then killing her husband, and how even after *that* God forgave him.

In the end, I just gritted my teeth and handed it to them.

Their reactions registered on the Richter scale.

"Three Ds!" my father shouted, throwing his camouflage hat onto the floor and kicking it. "Three Ds!"

That seemed to be all he could say. He didn't mention the two As, three Bs, or one C. His mind just seemed to *dillydally* around the three Ds.

Before my mother said one word, she crossed her legs, folded her arms, and glared at me, which was sign language for *"You are lucky I'm not holding a shotgun right now, son."*

"I don't know what to say that I haven't said a thousand times before, Virgil," said my mother, looking at my father.

"Well, son," said my father, "your mother—"

Mom interrupted. "I'd like to know what *you* think we should do, Matthew? Should we ground you? Would that do the trick? If we locked you in your room for thirty days, maybe you'd realize that this school thing isn't a game." She stopped talking and looked off into the distance like a soap-opera actress and shook her head. "I don't know what to say, Virgil, I really don't."

"Matthew," said my father, "you've—"

"Do you *even* care?" said my mother. "I want to know if you care or not. I can't believe you look at your grades and are satisfied with three Ds! Are you satisfied with three Ds? Are you?" She looked at my father. "What do you say to a boy who doesn't care? Do you have any idea what to say? Because I don't."

My father shrugged. "It seems to me, Matthew, that—"

"You're walking on thin ice, buddy! That's all I've got to say!" my mother said, lying through her teeth. She had more to say. "I wonder what God thinks about this. I wonder if he enjoys watching you throw away all the gifts and talents he's given you. Have you thought about that? Well, you might want to think it about. Do you think he's smiling right now, son?"

I shook my head, because any other response might have gotten me turned into a pillar of salt. But I didn't know if God was smiling or not.

I didn't know if God had a mouth or teeth or believed in the importance of an education. It was possible that his consequences for dillydallying my way to three Ds were the same as what the Old Testament recommended for disobeying one's parents: death by stoning. It didn't seem likely, but maybe God was up in heaven hoping my parents would take me outside, stand me up against a wall, and throw rocks at me.

Or *maybe,* because my blood was also their blood, he wanted them stoned too.

"That's enough, hon," said my father, "Let's give the boy a break."

"You're right," she said. "You know we love you, right?"

I did. I just didn't feel it at the moment.

My mother lectured me off and on for a week. My father carried three large rocks in his pocket for a couple of days. Overall, it wasn't too bad.

When I went into seventh grade, I stopped saving Jesus a seat on the bus. I did it cold turkey. Not because I had outgrown him or didn't want him to sit next to me, but because a girl named Chrissy wanted to sit there. She and I became boyfriend and girlfriend via a third party after seventy-two hours. Our whirlwind romance ended with our making a deal with Jesus, one that required him to sit between the two of us so we wouldn't be tempted to rub our arm hair against each other's.

Since she got on the bus first, she saved me a seat. After I arrived, we measured out six inches of seat space between our thighs, and that's where Jesus sat.

For the record, Jesus kept his end of the bargain.

Seven

Fundamentalism made me weird.

I wasn't alone. It made lots of people weird. But I think some people at my church believed that was the point, that somewhere in the Bible, Jesus declared, "Blessed are the weird." Our weirdness was a form of obedience unto God.

Things got peculiar for me early on. One Sunday morning my friend Jenny waltzed into our third-grade Sunday school class carrying a large, red and green plaid tin her mother had decorated with a fluorescent pink bow.

"Guess what, Matthew?" Jenny took off her puffy white church coat and threw it on the table in front of her. "Today's my birthday, and since it's on a Sunday, and my mother hates having birthday parties on Sundays, she made cookies for everybody in our class instead. Want to see them?"

Before I could say yes, Jenny tore off the bow and opened the lid. I looked inside.

"Oh, wow, Jenny," I said. "Your mom made cookies that look like Jesus."

Jenny's mother could make almost anything look like Jesus. Jenny brought most of her creations into school for show and tell. Her mother was best known for making Jesus-shaped throw pillows. Jenny told the class it was her mother's spiritual gift to take something not *naturally* about Jesus and come up with a creative way to make it artificially about him.

My mother did the same thing when she got the bright idea to throw Jesus a birthday party on Christmas Eve one year. In preparation for Jesus's birthday bash, Mom made a cake and put thirty-three birthday candles in it. After our church's Christmas Eve service, we came home and gathered around our dining-room table, lit the candles, and sang "Happy Birthday" to God's only Son.

After we finished singing, we stood really still and stared at the birthday cake for a couple of seconds. I think we were waiting to see who would blow out the candles, wondering if a mighty rushing wind would blow through the house and extinguish the flames.

Nothing happened.

Eventually, my brother-in-law leaned in and blew out the candles. Then he looked at all of us and said, "What? I didn't do anything."

The party wasn't as exciting as the Day of Pentecost, but the cake was good, and Mom was proud of herself, which was what being fundamentalist was all about. Pride went before a fall, but it was also something comfortable to lean on once in a while.

It was difficult to look at Jenny's Jesus-shaped cookies without wanting to pick one up so I could smell his face. I had never seen the face of Jesus look delicious before. I'd seen it look peaceful, patient, happy, and once even angry. But I'd never craved it with milk.

"Don't they look yummy?" Jenny asked. "Mom found Jesus cookie cutters in a Christian catalog." Jenny placed the lid back on the tin to keep her Jesus snacks from getting stale. "The frosting is homemade, but Mom had a hard time making the color brown, so his hair looks a little purple."

Now that she mentioned it, the cookies did resemble Tina Turner more than Jesus.

"Jenny, do you think Mrs. Snover will let us eat Jesus?"

I wasn't trying to be a downer, but I worried that it might be against our religion to digest the Son of God.

"Daddy wondered the same thing," said Jenny, "but Mom was like, 'Oh don't worry about it, hon! I used to be Catholic, and we ate Jesus all the time during communion.'"

My eyes widened. "Catholics *eat* Jesus?"

"That's what Mom said."

"That's disgusting. I'm happy I'm Baptist. I don't want to eat Jesus every Sunday."

When Mrs. Snover finished teaching us about Jesus's miracle of turning water into Welch's grape juice, the whole class sang "Happy Birthday" to Jenny, and I bit into Jesus's cheekbone.

He tasted good. So good that I saved some of his crumbs in a napkin just in case he wanted to come back to life in my pocket.

The older I got, the more I began to realize that the life I lived was not only difficult, it was strange and fearful. When I skipped reading my Bible or praying, I feared that God would punish me by making me crippled or killing my mother. On days that I hadn't read my Bible, I came home from school and called my mother at work.

"I just wanted to make sure you were all right," I told her once.

"I'm all right, sweetie," she said. "Is there something wrong?"

"No, I just wanted to make sure that God hadn't killed you."

"*What?* Why do you think God would do that?"

"I didn't read my Bible this morning, and sometimes I think he might punish me by letting you get into a car accident or something."

"Matthew, do you really think God would use *me* in your punishment?"

I didn't know the answer to that. I hoped he wouldn't, but I wasn't sure. People said odd things about God. They said he was in control, but then when a teenager was killed in a car accident or a young mother died of cancer, they said that he allowed those deaths to occur so other people would come to know Jesus.

That only made me fear God more, not have faith in him.

When I heard my mother pull into the garage, I prayed, *Thank you, God. I will never forget to read my Bible ever again. I promise. I will pray and read my Bible every day. I don't deserve to be a Christian. You have been so good to me, God, and I am so unfaithful. Thank you again for not hurting my mother. Tell Granddad hello. In Jesus's name, amen.*

To feel closer to God, I sometimes did unusual things—superstitious things. I couldn't walk past my Bible without rubbing its cover, as if subconsciously rubbing my skin against synthetic leather made me feel more Christian. If alone, sometimes I rubbed my Bible against my face, held it against my cheeks, or kissed the words *Holy Bible,* believing and sometimes even sensing that something miraculous was happening in that moment. While everybody I knew read the Bible, I was the only one who made out with it.

In fifth grade, I became a radical fan of the number seven. Since it was God's holy number, mentioned in the Bible more than seven hundred times, I did as many things as possible in series of seven. When I practiced my multiplication flashcards,

I repeated each of them out loud seven times. I believed that if I only repeated them six times, I wouldn't remember them, and if I did them eight times, God might think I didn't trust him. The same was true when I memorized spelling words or history facts, or when my mother told me my hair needed washing. *Seven* times.

When I shared my seven theory with my father, he shifted his eyes my direction and held them there until I felt uncomfortable and stupid.

"Buck, I think you're overdoing it a bit."

"But, Dad, how do you explain the story in the Bible about Naaman?" I asked. That was the only way to win an argument with my father—infiltrate the conversation with stories God wrote. "You remember that story, right? Naaman wanted to be healed, and God told the prophet Elisha to tell him to dunk himself in the Jordan River seven times. And what happened? God took away Naaman's leprosy."

Dad's forehead crinkled, which normally caused me to cry *uncle*. But not that time.

"Or what about God telling Joshua to march around the wall of Jericho once a day for seven days? *Huh?* And then on the seventh day, he told them to march around it seven times. And you know the rest of the story—the walls came tumblin' down."

I considered standing up in the middle of our living room and singing the Sunday school song that went with that story, thinking it might accentuate my point. But I decided it would be unimpressive since it required at least three people to make the "tumblin' down" hand motions seem authentic in relation to the death and devastation that had occurred.

"And of course," I said, "God created the world in six days and then he rested on the *seventh*. Six plus one equals seven. What do you think about my idea now?"

"I don't know, Buck," he said. "I think you're taking those stories out of context, and I don't want you to be disappointed when it doesn't work out for you like it did for the people in the Bible."

My father was one of the few fundamental Baptists I knew who actually valued context when reading the Bible. Most people took every word to heart. I knew people who, if there was a disagreement, searched for a way to apply King Solomon's solution when forced to decide which of two mothers a baby belonged to.

"Maybe we should just cut this thing in two," somebody suggested when two of my friends were arguing about which of them had brought the *signed* Cal Ripken Jr. baseball card to Sunday school.

However, both of them yelled, "No, don't cut it," which wasn't how the Bible story went. But Solomon's wisdom still proved helpful, since the Sunday school teacher awarded the card to the kid who *didn't* use an expletive when yelling.

I also knew people who, when lost and alone, remembered how God led the children of Israel in the wilderness and then looked up, anticipating a cloud of fire to guide them home or at least to the nearest gas station.

Dad believed that every word of the Bible had at one time

come out of the mouth of God, but he thought applying those miraculous events to the happenings in our lives should be handled with care and common sense. Although my father thought God was capable of creating a cloud of fire, he didn't find it all that necessary, considering we had road maps and compasses. And unlike the Israelites' situation in the desert, our getting lost hadn't been God's idea to begin with.

"You don't have leprosy, Buck," he said, "so it's difficult for me to think that the promise God made to Naaman instantly applies to you. But that's just how I think about it. You think about it the way you want to, all right?"

He picked up the remote control and unmuted the television, an action I knew meant we were finished with our discussion. The last word always belonged to Dad, unless he was arguing with my mother. Even if it didn't happen when the two of them were in the same room, Mom always got the last word.

Going against the wisdom of my father felt wrong. Even when I thought he was contradicting God, he *usually* ended up being right.

And I don't remember thinking my father was weird.

When I became a teenager, I realized it wasn't so much that I was weird but that fundamentalism was weird. I was just a by-product. I learned that in my tenth-grade Bible class.

My teacher, Mr. Shenmeister, looked like the Pillsbury Doughboy. He was short, round, and soft, and had dimples as deep as moon craters. But despite looking as though he should be standing naked next to some crescent rolls, he was one of my favorite teachers. There was something different about Mr. Shenmeister's form of fundamentalism. While he lived just as holy as any of the other men who heard from God on a regular basis, the messages he received from the Almighty didn't make him mean-spirited or better than everybody else. Instead, they seemed to make him compassionate and kind. He was the first man of God I knew who put his love for people before his love for rules.

During one of his more accessible lectures about God's Word, an in-depth study of the ten most hated individuals in the Bible, we were studying the obvious number one— Satan—when I raised my hand.

"Mr. Shenmeister, God created Lucifer, right?"

Before answering, he looked at me as if he regretted pointing at my hand. "That's right, Matthew. God created Lucifer. He was one of his original angels."

Walking out from behind his podium, he folded his hands in front of his belly, as if he was hiding something.

"Well, Mr. Shenmeister, do you think God knew that Lucifer would one day become Satan? In other words, did he know that by making him, he was, well, going to wreak havoc on the world?"

"Matthew, I believe God knows absolutely everything. He's sovereign. So, yes, that means he knew what Satan would eventually become."

"Then why did he create him?"

A couple of my classmates looked at me like I was asking

a forbidden question, as if by wondering about such things, I had set out a welcome mat for Satan to come inside my head, sit down on the couch, and feel comfortable enough to pass gas. Even Mr. Shenmeister, the only fundamentalist pastor/teacher who didn't approve of shoving hymnals between unmarried couples who sat too close in church, looked at me as though he was worried about my soul.

But my question wasn't a cynical one. I really wanted to know the answer.

"Matthew, it's difficult to understand, I know, but it comes down to trust. Trusting that God always knows best. Sometimes asking why is a good thing, even a needed thing. But sometimes asking those questions just opens us up to feeling unsure about our faith. And Satan is cunning like that. He likes to confuse young thinkers like yourself with big questions. He'd love to get you to blame God for all the problems in the world."

And then, as an afterthought, he looked right at me. "Some of this stuff I teach is weird, Matthew, and hard to understand. Lots of things the Bible talks about are different. But just because something's weird doesn't mean it isn't true." His face became less serious than before. "It just means it's weird."

The bell rang, and I put everything I needed to take home in my book bag. Right before throwing my bag onto my shoulder, I picked up my Bible and slid my hand across its cover. I looked to see if anybody was watching me.

When the coast was clear, I kissed the word *Holy* before tossing the Bible in my bag.

Fertile Soil

I thought everybody who didn't go to my church was lost. Not physically misplaced like the people whose pictures were printed on milk cartons or hung in post offices, but far worse. They were spiritually lost—blind, ignorant, and seemingly incapable of seeing the mysterious God signs he had graciously sprinkled amid our surroundings. Take trees, for instance.

Pastor Nolan once described God as being like the roots of a tree, its foundation and source of nourishment. The leaves of a tree represented us, people who would crumple up and die without the root's nourishment.

"How do leaves get what they need from the roots?" Pastor Nolan stood behind his pulpit, waiting for one of us to blurt out the answer. "It's so obvious, church. Does anybody know?"

Somebody in the back of the auditorium yelled, "The tree trunk."

"Exactly." Pastor Nolan waved his hands in the air. "Thank God for the tree trunk. Don't you see? The tree trunk represents Jesus, our only way to receive the nourishment we need from God. Without Jesus, we die."

Pastor Nolan's analogy made sense to me, but I didn't think this was a perfect explanation until I took it a step further and considered how Jesus had died on a cross, a cross that was once a tree trunk.

After that, I assumed if a lost person would simply consider the tree, it would be impossible for them to remain oblivious to their need for Jesus. To me, it was like a blinking road sign. *Believe in Jesus. Believe in Jesus.* But people missed it all the time. I'd tell one of my lost friends what I saw in the tree and they'd *still* refuse to confess their sins.

"So, you want to ask Jesus into your heart?" I asked an acquaintance once after I had shared my flawless tree analogy. "You could do it right now. It's easy."

"I don't want to."

"Why not?"

"For one thing, we're at the Dover Mall, Matthew. The *mall.* There are hundreds of people around."

"Who cares what they think? This is important, man. We're talking about heaven or hell."

"And furthermore, I'm pretty sure that tree we're looking at is made of fiberglass and plastic."

"Yeah, but you missed my point. I'm just using it as an example. Of a *real* tree." I stopped talking for a moment and looked around the mall, waiting for some of the people in our area to leave. "Are you sure you don't want to ask Jesus into your heart? There aren't that many people around right now."

"No, man, I don't want to."

"Nobody will see you doing it. You don't even have to close your eyes. I'll mumble the prayer."

"No. Can we talk about something else, please? Or I'm gonna tell my mother what you've been talking to me about."

It wasn't easy walking around in public and seeing so many unfound people in the world. It was like having a sixth sense, one that constantly told me, *"You could save that person. He needs to hear about Jesus."* If I ignored its warning, it laid a guilt trip on me. *"So you don't care about that person's soul, huh? It doesn't bother you that she might burn in hell for eternity? Okay, I see how it is. You might feel differently if she gets killed in a car accident on her way home."*

Sometimes I could turn off the voice in my head. I could walk away without caring enough to say anything, but doing that came with consequences. For a few days I saw that person's face in my mind, surrounded by the flames of hell, covered in sweat, and then I would feel guilty about not talking to them.

Pastor Nolan told us that when we got to heaven, during an event he called the Judgment Seat of Christ, we would be punished for every occasion we'd had a chance to tell somebody about Jesus and didn't. "And do you know what will happen, church? You will stand before almighty God on Judgment Day, and one by one, every person you failed to share Jesus with will walk into God's heavenly courtroom.

And God will say to each of them, 'Is this the man who failed to tell you about my Son?' And they will point you out, and God will put their blood on your hands, and you will not be able to wash it off."

I am three years older than my sister Elisabeth. During that particular sermon, she sat next to me, obviously not paying attention. "Did you hear what he just said?" I whispered.

"No, I was counting how many times my name is mentioned in the Bible. What did he say?"

"That God is going to put other people's blood on our hands, the people we haven't talked to about Jesus."

"Are you serious? That's gross."

"I know. I'll faint if that happens. You know how I am with blood. I can't even watch reruns of *Hogan's Heroes*."

While Pastor Nolan said his closing prayer, Elisabeth leaned over and put her mouth near my ear. "Have you ever told Julie about Jesus?"

"Of course. I've known her since we were three."

"I don't think I have."

"Really?"

"Yeah, and I really don't want her blood on my hands."

"Well, just talk to her then."

"Maybe I'll call her when we get home. Remind me."

"I will."

"What do I say to her?"

"You can use my tree story. I'll explain it to you on the way home."

"Cool."

■ ■ ■

My father loved nature, and I believed he knew more about it than any other person in my life. He worked at Kent County's Soil Conservation Service. It was a government job he'd kept since he was eighteen years old.

Dad was proud of being a part of America's working middle class. Every dollar he put into his savings account added another brick to the wall he hoped separated him from how his father had managed life, money, and family.

Dad grew up poor, and he rarely talked about the hardships of his childhood. He seemed only able to recollect the memories that made people laugh or shake their heads in amazement. Sometimes he seemed embarrassed even hinting at how poor his family was. He only brought it up during discussions about money, usually with my mother.

"Did you need new shoes?" he asked whenever my mother brought home a new set of clogs, sandals, or tennis shoes.

"They were on sale, Virgil."

"Hon," Dad said, "you would buy a mad dog if it were on sale."

"Virgil, that makes about as much sense as"—Mom thought for moment, hoping the perfect simile would come to mind—"as...as...as I don't know what."

"You know, Carole, when I was a boy..."

My father started talking about being eight years old and having to go two years without a new pair of shoes, despite the holes in them and their being two sizes too small, because his parents couldn't afford a new pair. Or he reminded us of a Christmas morning when he was twelve and only received some tube socks and underwear. When he was feeling particularly vulnerable, he told us about the two and a half years he lived in a house with such poor insulation that during much of the winter he lay in bed shivering and unable to sleep.

I always believed Dad stopped short of telling us the whole story. Maybe he couldn't, or he believed his point was made just teasing us with a headline or two. My mother knew the parts of Dad's narrative we didn't, but she only vaguely referred to them when we were mad at our father for being a cheapskate or suggesting we were—*God forbid*—poor.

During the summer months, while I was out of school, my father sometimes let me ride along on his afternoon appointments. Most of Dad's work involved meetings with farmers. Riding in my father's work truck made me feel important, like I had a purpose. I took along a tablet of paper and a pencil because I enjoyed pretending it was my responsibility to write a report on the conditions of the farms we visited.

There are three trees along the driveway, I'd write. *They look like they need water and fertilizer. I see a squirrel sitting in one of the trees. Seven geese are sitting on the pond. That's two less than last year. One is bigger than the others. He must be the boy goose.*

I'd eventually get bored reporting on nature and begin writing other things. I wrote poems or prayers, or on bad days I wrote down all the things I didn't like about my friends.

Willie lies about everything. Penney is mean, and I think that's why God made her fat. I don't think Geoff is saved.

On the way to these meetings, when I wasn't writing, Dad taught me about agriculture. I loved my father's impromptu lectures about the importance of conservation. He spoke about soil the same way he spoke about God, with reverence and awe. Nothing disgusted him more than driving down a road and finding signs of good farmland being washed away.

"You see that gully right there, Buck?"

I looked out my window at a mini Grand Canyon along the road.

"That right there is not good," he said, making a mental note to visit that farmer. "You see how the dirt looks like it's been moving? It has. That means every time it rains, we lose soil. Good soil. It ends up polluting the Chesapeake Bay." Dad then told me how he'd solve the problem. "A good waterway with some thick grass would fix that right up and save the Bay from all the pesticides these farmers use."

Our lives depended on the Bay. My father believed the Chesapeake was our county's greatest resource. That's why he was so passionate about protecting it. He loved the Bay because it not only provided a way of life for many of the people living in our small farming and fishing community, but it also acted as a protective shield, one that kept our land free and clear of the sex offenders, alcoholics, and lunatics we assumed lived in Baltimore. "We need to keep those crazies on the *other* side of the Bay," Dad would say.

My favorite part about going to work with Dad was meeting the contractors he worked with. My father described the men and women who rode around in excavators as if they were their own race, a culture of people redeemed only by their ability to dig very exact holes in the ground. My father rarely allowed me to see these heathens up close, lest one of them use God's name as an adjective. But the churchless lives of these people fascinated me in a *National Geographic* sort of way.

I felt guilty about my interest, but it was true. I looked at them and wondered what it must be like to exist without a conscience. Such freedom, I thought. I bet they drank the contents of beer cans, played poker on Tuesday nights, slept in until one o'clock on Sunday afternoon, and watched *Three's Company* and *Thundercats* whether their parents were in the room or not. I was curious what it felt like not to be completely aware of every detail of your life. To just live and not care about the consequences. Deep down, a part of me hoped it felt like irritable bowel syndrome, because then my church would be right about the pain associated with sin. But a part of me feared they were content and happy, and that made my stomach ache.

"Buck, this boy you're going to meet today," my father said, "acts like a nutcase half the time, but he'll work. Boy, will he work. I've never seen a harder worker in all my life."

Dad loved work almost as much as he loved going to church, and few things impressed him more than a person's work ethic. But it had to be a specific kind of work to count. It couldn't include studying, a typewriter, or a musical instrument.

You had to do the kind of work that made you sweat like

a fat man and want to go to bed at 7:30 every evening. My father admired that kind of person the way other people admired those with doctorates in history and philosophy or celebrities who had their own get-rich-quick schemes.

I met Tuck in the middle of a cornfield on a day that felt like God was giving us a taste of what hell might be like if he installed a humidifier. Tuck saw Dad pulling up in the work truck and climbed down from his tractor. He was shorter than I expected, but he compensated for his undersized legs by walking briskly toward us. His face was red and leathery from years working under the sun, and his blue work shirt was tattered at the tail and looked like it had been dipped in motor oil. Despite Dad telling me Tuck was wealthy and successful, I pictured him coming out of a cave that morning, beating his fists against his chest like a gorilla.

"Oh no," yelled Tuck. "Look who the devil dragged in. You've come to give me crap about something, haven't you, Virgil?"

Tuck's voice sounded serious, and he had enough dirt under his fingernails to pot a chrysanthemum. I didn't want to shake his hand, but I realized my judgment was hasty when I saw a smile appear on my father's face. Dad was known around town for that grin.

"Yeah, yeah," said my father. It was obvious he'd heard Tuck say that before. "You know better than to think the devil had anything to do with me coming to see you."

"Oh yeah, that's right," Tuck said. "I'm the one who spends too much time with the devil. Not you."

They both laughed.

When he was close enough, Dad grabbed Tuck's hand and shook it hard. "How you doing, Tuck?"

"I'm hot," he said, then added, "Maybe this is God giving me a little practice for eternity."

Dad just shook his head. "Hey, Tuck, have you ever met my son, Matthew?"

"I don't believe I have," he said. "Howdy, son. It's good to meet you. I'm sure you know this already, but you got yourself a good daddy. He talks about Jesus too much, but I like him anyway."

I shook Tuck's hand, doing my best to mimic my father's stable grip, and then when he wasn't looking, wiped my fingers on my blue jeans. "Good to meet you, sir," I said.

"Has your father told you that he thinks I'm going to hell?" Tuck slapped his knee and howled like a coyote.

I assumed Tuck's question was rhetorical, and it would have been impolite to tell him my father had mentioned a time or two that he believed Tuck was going to bust the gates of hell wide open. I'd only known the man for thirty seconds, and I concurred with my father.

"Son, your daddy has been trying to win my soul for Jesus for six years. Maybe more. Ain't that right, Virgil? To tell you the truth, he makes a good point. Jesus might actually do me some good. But all my friends are going to be in hell, and I wouldn't want to miss a party."

"You keep on talking, Tuck," my father said, still grinning. "One of these days you might wish you'd listened to me."

"Virgil, you could be right," said Tuck, "but I figure if there's a God, you know he damned my soul a long time ago."

Dad shook his head as if he had nothing to add.

As Tuck and my father talked about the type of grass that needed to be planted in the waterway, I sat in my father's truck and envisioned Tuck and his friends partying in hell. Maybe he was right that Budweiser would be a sponsor on Tuesdays and all four of the Beatles would reunite for an underworld tour. "So don't go trying to *save* Ringo, Virgil," Tuck said. "He's the only one of the four who might be tempted to sway your direction."

Tuck's version of hell sounded nothing like Pastor Nolan's. The way Pastor Nolan talked about hell, it didn't sound like anything close to a party. "You've probably seen the lava that pours out of a volcano, right?" he asked us once. "If you have, then you've seen what hell is going to be like. Think of it like a tidal wave of scorching hot lava."

I thought about the heads of Tuck and his friends bobbing up and down in hell's red, steamy current. And then the truck door opened and my father climbed inside.

On the way back to his office, my father listened to talk radio, and I counted how many vultures I saw in the sky. Eventually Dad turned the radio off. "Tuck is quite the character, isn't he?"

"I'll say. Why didn't you get angry at him when he talked like that about hell?"

"Oh, there's no sense in getting angry with anybody," said Dad. "He has every right to believe what he believes. It makes me sad, but at the end of the day I don't want to be angry with anybody."

"Yeah, but Pastor Nolan isn't that way," I said. "He would have put Tuck in his place or else."

"Or else what?" said Dad. "Lose a friend? I'm probably the only person in that boy's life who even mentions God. Whether he becomes a Christian or not, I think I'm there for a reason. I don't *know* the reason right now, and I'm okay with that. But mark my word, Buck, God has a way of making things right."

That summer my family took a vacation to Yellowstone National Park. It was the year after the park suffered the loss of thousands of acres due to fires. On our second day there, while walking one of the trails, we came upon a meadow that was almost entirely black.

"Look at that." My mother could hardly believe her eyes. "I don't think I've ever seen anything quite like this. How many acres is that meadow, do you think?"

"Oh gosh, probably a thousand or more." My father gazed out across the field and then, a few moments later, looked down at the ground in front of him. "How about that? Hey, guys, come here. Look at this." He pointed to a spot on the ground right in front of his foot. "Isn't that *something*?"

There, in the middle of the black was a speck of something green, something alive.

"Dad, is that a baby tree?" I got down on my knees and put my eyes close to the ground. "It is. Dad, that's a seedling. That's amazing."

I inspected the ground further and found numerous specks of green popping up in the middle of the black. "Isn't that cool, Dad?"

"It's a miracle." My mother pushed her sunglasses up on the top of her head. "I bet in a year or two you won't even be able to tell there was a fire. Isn't that right, Virgil?"

"Absolutely. I bet this meadow will be entirely green by next summer."

My eyes scanned the meadow one last time. "Those seedlings are amazing."

"Yep, that's God for you, son."

Satan Rules!

My ninth-grade algebra teacher was a very tall man who enjoyed wearing his pants hiked up to just below his nipples. That's how he was dressed one day when he walked into class, shaking his head and mumbling to himself. He stood at the front of the classroom and said, "Well, it's official. America is going to hell in a prom dress."

The manner in which he said it made me wonder if he was the one who decided such matters.

"I didn't think it could get worse than Michael Jackson and his crotch-grabbing immorality, kids." Mr. Nelg put one hand on his kidneys, leaned against his podium, and stroked the teacher's edition of our algebra book.

"I mean, I've seen a lot of sinful stuff happen in my lifetime. The Beatles, for example. It wasn't long ago when one of them compared himself to Jesus, which irritated me to no end. Do you know how mad I got? I could have punched a hole right through that chalkboard. That's how mad I was. They don't want to get me too mad. They don't. And then there's those good-for-nothing liberals on *M.A.S.H.*—have you seen the mockery of God and America that happens on that show? It blows my mind how far we've come in America. And I worry for you guys."

Even though we had no idea what Mr. Nelg was talking about, none of us took what he said too seriously. He worried about a lot of odd things. The year before, he told us a union of witches was gathering on New Year's Eve to pray that all Christians be removed from the world.

"Yes, witches have unions," he said. "You can thank Thomas Jefferson for that one." None of us knew what that meant, but we figured it had something to do with his belief in an underground secret society whose main goal was to "downsize Christianity."

Most of us had learned not to care about the things he claimed, and that only made Mr. Nelg worry more.

"You know that song 'We Are the World'?" he asked us in the middle of a Christmas party. "You mark my word, that song is setting the stage for a one-world government, and it will bring about the Tribulation! *By 1989.* Mark that down. You think I'm kidding you. I'm not, kids. This is legit stuff."

Some of us got nervous once in a while, but we eventually recognized that Mr. Nelg was just an algebra teacher who probably owned a police scanner and had a bunch of overdue library books and a VHS copy of *The Wizard of Oz* on his nightstand.

"Satan's at work, kids. He really is. And this weekend he is working double time." Mr. Nelg told us he wanted to lead us in a prayer for America. Not knowing what the coming weekend would bring, I assumed he was going to pray against our country's addiction to sex, foul language, violence, partial nudity, and *Dynasty*, which was Satan's idea of a combo.

According to anybody who was *anybody* at my church, the devil was a cunning individual. But he was also a simple creature. For instance, nothing made him happier than luring our young minds in front of the television to watch *Knots Landing*.

Hollywood was on his side.

Mr. Nelg asked us once, "Kids, would you eat a brownie if I told you I put a tablespoon of poop in the batter?"

We shook our heads and voiced our disgust at the thought of such an idea. "*Wait.* I only put a tablespoon. You probably wouldn't even taste it amid all of the brownie's fudgy goodness." We still said no. "Well, then, what about the entertainment you watch? Some of you don't mind eating poo when you're watching movies or television. That's what you're doing when you watch PG movies or *The Cosby Show.* Sure, there's only a *little* 'poo in the batter,' but still, you watch it."

I thought about the time I'd let myself stumble by watching the movie *Big.* Mr. Nelg was right. I had eaten poo. His illustration made me feel so guilty that I bowed my head right there and confessed to God my love of fecal matter in entertainment.

Satan was clever, I thought.

I didn't understand much about Satan back then. It was hard to think of the devil as an actual person, somebody who could run, hide, do somersaults if he wanted, and manage the career of Aerosmith. I was told he wasn't *exactly* flesh and blood, but those same people claimed he wasn't a spirit either. He was the most beautiful of all angels. *Fallen.* Forsaken by his own free will to be just like God. Nobody liked admitting this—but he was like us, except he had better publicity.

My church told us he couldn't be more powerful than God, but still, Satan was influential. He caused people in South America to become Catholic, and in India, he deified cattle. People pointed to the place in the Bible that called him the "prince of the air." Some people at my church thought that meant he was in charge of radio and television broadcasts. Others thought that meant he ruled over everything that used oxygen to survive. Sometimes I wanted to live in a vacuum.

We went to great lengths to keep the devil at bay.

In seventh grade, I went to Bill Bentley's thirteenth birthday party. The plan was to celebrate the day with cake, ice cream, and an afternoon watching the movie *Ben-Hur.* I was the only kid there who had never seen *Ben-Hur,* which, according to Bill's mother, was a travesty.

"You are going to *love* it, Matthew," Mrs. Bentley told me as I helped her set up the VCR while we waited for Bill and his other friends to finish eating lunch. "*Love it.* It's one of my favorite stories of all time. Every Christian should see this movie. Charlton is delightful. It's very inspirational."

"There's one *bad* part in it," said Amy, Bill's ten-year-old sister, who was sitting on the couch.

"A *bad* part?" I asked. "In *Ben-Hur*?

"Amy Lynn Bentley," yelled Mrs. Bentley, "what did I tell you?" Her eyes zapped Amy back against the couch and held her there. "What did I tell you? Amy, look at me."

The room stopped. For that moment, the only two people allowed to say anything were Mrs. Bentley and Amy. Baptists rarely feared disciplining their children in front of other Baptists. Rearing up a child in the way he or she should go was as commonplace among fundamentalists as homophobia or whistling "Amazing Grace" while completing household chores. My role in that situation was to look off into a corner of the room and pretend not to be there until the disciplinary action was complete. Once Mrs. Bentley finished pointing her child in the holier direction, it was my job to make sure nothing seemed awkward about what I had witnessed.

"Well, Amy, are you going to tell me?" Mrs. Bentley repeated a third time. "What did I ask you not to do?"

I was tempted to answer the question myself. Or perhaps mouth to Amy what she should say to her mother. *Mom, I'm so sorry. I must have had a lapse of good Christian judgment, and instead of heeding your wise counsel not to mention* Ben-Hur's *immoral segment, I listened to my own sin-wracked flesh and vocalized the very thing you asked me to keep quiet. I'm sorry. I confess my sin unto you and unto God.*

But I didn't say a word. I knelt on their living-room floor and stared into a corner, where I saw a brick somebody had covered with a needlepoint pattern that spelled "Bentley" in a vibrant array of colors. We had one of those bricks. Ours had a duck on the front.

Then, just when I thought Mrs. Bentley's eyes would push her daughter into the crevices of the sofa with the lost pennies, bobby pins, and a dirty white sock, Amy's will cracked under the pressure.

"I wasn't supposed to talk about the bad part," she said.

"Thank you, Amy," said Mrs. Bentley. "That wasn't so hard, now was it?"

The room got quiet for a few seconds, almost awkward. But I saved the moment, the party, the day. "Amy, what's your favorite Bible story?"

A few minutes later, we were sucked into the beginning scenes of *Ben-Hur.* Bill and I sat on one couch. His other two friends sat on the floor in front of the television. About two minutes into the movie, Amy pranced in and plopped down between Bill and me.

"Has the bad part happened?" she whispered to Bill.

"It's coming up, I think," he whispered back.

The bad part? I thought. *What could possibly be bad about a movie that looked like it could have been made when Lincoln was president?* But since the *bad* part had already caused enough drama that afternoon, I just watched and waited and hoped I noticed it when it happened.

"Should I get Mom?" asked Amy.

"Nah, I'm going to yell for her in a bit," Bill said.

"Okay, but you might give her the warning."

"Mom," yelled Bill. "The bad part is coming in a minute or two."

There was no answer.

"Mom! The bad part is coming." He looked at Amy. "Where is she?"

"MOM!" screamed Amy in unison with her brother. "Come quick! The bad part is almost on!"

Still, there was no answer. Then, a minute later, we heard the toilet flush.

"Oh," said Bill. "Amy…can you get her?"

When Amy left, I leaned toward Bill. "Hey," I whispered. "What's the bad part?"

Bill's eyes got wide. "Um, well, boobs." His face turned red. "Sorry, maybe I should have said 'bosoms.'"

"In *Ben-Hur*?" I said. "There are boobs in *Ben-Hur*? Isn't Jesus in this movie?"

"Yes, he is. But he's not alone."

"In *Ben-Hur*?" I said again. "They show boobs in *Ben-Hur*?"

"Yes!" said Bill. "Stop saying it."

Amy ran into the room. "Mom's on her way."

We heard the toilet flush again, but we pretended not to.

"MOM!" screamed Bill. "Are you coming?"

"I'm coming, baby!" came a voice from the bathroom. "I'm gonna be there in a second."

"I'd hurry, Mom!" yelled Bill. "We're almost at that scene!"

Meanwhile, Judah Ben-Hur was getting ready to visit his mother and sister. At this point in the movie, he's happy and not running around bare-chested. But it wouldn't be much longer before poor Ben-Hur's life took a drastic turn toward insanity.

"MOM! IT'S COMING!" shouted Bill. "Hurry!"

"I'm coming," the bathroom voice said again. Mrs. Bentley flushed the toilet a third time. We heard her washing her hands.

"IT'S ALMOST ON, MOM!" Bill screamed.

By this time, I had decided I really wanted to see the bad part. But I was pretty sure Mrs. Bentley wasn't going to let that happen.

Mrs. Bentley opened the bathroom door. We heard fast footsteps. Moments later, we saw her running as fast as she could down the hallway.

"Mom! Hurry!" cheered Amy.

"Yeah, hurry!" echoed Bill.

She turned at the end of the hallway and ran into the living room, jumped over the dog, and took a flying leap over a leather ottoman. Then she dropped onto the floor, right in front of the television.

"This is the scene, Mom!" yelled Bill.

She was just in time. We watched as Ben-Hur's sister walked through a door. Mrs. Bentley was ready. As soon as we saw the sister, Mrs. Bentley placed two of her fingers over the top half of the girl's dress. As the young girl walked down a staircase, so did Mrs. Bentley's fingers, following the girl's breasts all the way down the stairs and then holding them there until the scene finished. Thirty seconds later, the bad part ended. I felt like I should stand and applaud Mrs. Bentley. She was magnificent, by far the best part of the movie for me.

Never in my life had I seen such dedication from a mother trying to rid her home of the craftiness of Satan. It bordered on psychotic, but it brought a tear to my eye.

Boobs were just one of the many reasons I wasn't allowed to see movies in a theater.

I learned early on that theaters were dark, evil places where drugs got sold and bodily fluids exchanged. With that kind of mental picture, I never really wanted to go to the theater, and when I saw long lines in front of the box office at the Dover Mall, I became grossed out imagining those poor sinners spitting into each other's mouths. When you sit under the preaching of a pastor who week after week makes a multiplex sound as healthy as an STD clinic in Thailand, it sinks in and becomes your reality.

I remember one of the kids at church telling me that his mother took him to see *Bambi* at a movie theater.

"She did?" I asked. "Was it disgusting?"

"Nope," he said. "It was so cool. They served popcorn, lemonade, and gobstoppers!"

"Did you spit at anybody?"

He looked at me funny, rolled his eyes, and told me I was weird.

He must be a new Baptist, I thought.

When I got home, I asked my mother why I couldn't see *Bambi* at the movie theater. "It's a kids' movie. One of the kids at church went to see it."

"I know it's a kids' movie," she told me, putting her hands around my shoulders. "I actually saw it at the theater a long time ago, before I was saved. But honey, after we became Christians, your father and I decided we didn't want our money supporting that dirty, sin-filled Hollywood. And when we give them money, even when it's just for a kids' movie, like *Bambi*—and it really is a cute movie—the devil takes our hard-earned money and he makes dirty movies with it."

"Oh," I said.

My mother was good at explaining things to me. Not perfect, but what mother is? Mom usually stopped what she was doing, gave me her mostly undivided attention, and answered my questions as honestly as she thought appropriate for a kid my age. She rarely made me feel like I was asking a stupid question.

I think it was important to my mom that I understood why we did the things we did, and why we didn't do other things—the latter being often more confusing for me. She and my father believed that the things we did and didn't do weren't simply a list of household rules. They were much more important than that. No matter how silly or pointless they seemed, because my parents believed our Baptist dos and don'ts brought a smile to God's face, they mattered on a level I wasn't fully capable of understanding.

At least, not then.

A few months later Pastor Nolan proved my mother's theory about Hollywood correct. Or at least, he supported it. He preached to my junior-church class and told us that it didn't matter if a person went to see a porn movie or *Bambi;* all of the money eventually trickled down to fund people who made the X-rated stuff.

I didn't know what pornography was, but the way Pastor Nolan described it, I was pretty sure miniskirts were involved.

I was a very visual kid. I didn't have a photographic memory, but if I saw a picture or movie that intrigued me, it got stuck inside my brain and worked its way into my dream world. Satan liked kids with big imaginations. For that reason, my parents were protective about what I watched.

When I was seven, my church rented a movie screen and showed the Christian thriller *A Thief in the Night.* Even though the devil had nothing to do with the making of that movie, my mother didn't like the idea of my seeing it. But she warmed up to it after learning it was loosely based on the book of Revelation. I suppose she didn't think it was necessary or very Christian of her to protect me from a movie with a screenplay practically written by God.

After we watched the film, she regretted her decision. My mother was horrified by the conclusion. It ended with a young girl who looked like Marcia Brady waiting in line to be executed because she wouldn't take the mark of the beast.

Instead, she had decided to take a happier route and follow Jesus, but that meant she would face death by decapitation. The final scene showed the poor thing tied down to a guillotine, screaming at the top of her lungs, "I'll take the mark! I'll take the mark! Don't kill me!" And then an earthquake happened, which released the blade, which made "Marcia" scream bloody murder, and then, just before the blade sliced off her head, the screen went black. (To be continued.)

Upon seeing that movie, I slept with my parents for three weeks because I kept having nightmares that I was tied to a guillotine and getting my head chopped off into a bucket.

My mother refused to let me see the sequel until I turned nine. Even that was a rather disastrous mistake. One of the characters was an old, fat, "worldly" preacher named Matthew Turner. When the man said his name, half the church turned around in their pews to see where I was. Some of them smiled. A few of them waved. Others gave me the thumbs-up, as if it was somehow cool that Jesus had decided to leave me behind on earth to get chased around by creatures that were half female and half scorpion. Needless to say, I freaked out, mostly because I wondered if the old man depicted in the movie was a prophecy about me.

That guy's face remained in my brain for a month. Finally, my father, with his matter-of-fact wisdom, helped me figure out a way to ensure I would not end up being the guy in the movie. "Buck, did you see how fat he was?" my father asked. "Just don't ever get fat, and you'll never be that guy. You've got nothing to worry about."

■ ■ ■

By teaching the various ways Satan utilized rock'n'roll to destroy people's lives, a man called Patch the Pirate came to our church one Sunday to inspire us with fear.

I found the Jesus-loving pirate impressive. While other people seemed enthused by the black patch that covered his left eye and his perfect diction when he enunciated the word *arrgh,* what really impressed me was how much sinful dirt he had dug up on Whitney Houston.

"Every Christian in this auditorium needs to listen to me." Patch raised his right eyebrow and ogled every face in the room. "You probably didn't know this, since most people think of her as an innocent, talented, and harmless entertainer, but Whitney Houston is *not* a saint. In fact, I wouldn't let that woman's voice anywhere near my church. Do you want to know why? Because Miss *Innocent* Whitney Houston promotes breaking two of the Ten Commandments."

Patch raised his right eyebrow again and *arrghed* at us. "That's the truth. I can tell that a good many of you didn't know this about her. But just maybe you've heard this song of hers…"

Patch motioned to the sound guy to hit play. Seconds later, the words and melody of Whitney's "Saving All My Love for You" filled the church auditorium. Six Whitney-syllables later, Patch rolled his right eye and scrunched up his nose. "Okay, that's enough. Turn it off. My soul is so in touch with Jesus that it actually hurts me to hear such godlessness.

Christian, you might think that's just a pretty voice, but you know what I'm hearing?"

Patch turned around and looked at Pastor Nolan. "You know what I hear, Preacher?"

He spun on one foot and put his good eyeball on the congregation. "The *voice of Satan*! Yep, I hear Satan in that sweet little voice. Satan sounds so good, doesn't he, using her voice to tell people that there's nothing wrong with coveting a man's body? That's rule breaker number one! But guess what the catch is? The man's body she covets is already married to another woman." He jumped around on the stage for a moment, then said, "Preacher, can you tell your congregation what Miss Houston is *really* singing about?"

"Sounds to me like adultery."

"Bingo. Rule breaker number two! Am I right?"

Even my mother was shocked by this information. She thought Whitney had a beautiful voice. She'd fallen in love with it during the 1988 Olympics when she heard her sing, "One Moment in Time."

That evening we learned lots of things about the satanic lifestyles of famous singers. We learned that Ozzy Osbourne ate small mammals for breakfast, and one of his songs included the lyrics, "I hate God, but I love Satan." But only when you played the song in reverse.

"I'd prove it to you if I had the right sound equipment with me," Patch said, "but I'm telling you the truth—I heard 'I hate God' with my own ears. Sounded just like demons talking. Awful experience."

I once heard Madonna's "Like a Virgin" played backward, but I didn't hear any messages. It just sounded like she was singing in Icelandic. I thought she could have been proclaiming her love of Satan in a different tongue.

"Can you tell me who has the time to sit and listen to records in reverse?" My mother made an excellent point, so much that I wrote it down in my Bible. "Besides, if somebody does have that kind of time, why would they sit around and listen to rock songs backward? That doesn't make sense. I would never have known or cared what Ozzy sang when his songs are played in reverse if that Pirate hadn't told anybody. I've never even heard Ozzy sing before."

According to Patch, the heart-pounding drumbeats made rock music dangerous. "The beats you hear on the radio every single day are the same ones that, *in Africa,* conjure up evil spirits," he said confidently. "I've actually interviewed African missionaries who tell me that, as soon as the gangs or tribes or whatever they call them get their drums going, the natives dance and take off their clothes. Compare *that* to what happens at some of these rock concerts, especially the ones sponsored by Budweiser."

To further prove his point, Patch had three toddlers in diapers—volunteers, he called them—carried onto the stage.

"Now you watch this," said Patch, winking at the sound guy. As soon as the eighties dance beat began playing, two of the three toddlers began shaking their bodies to the beat. Those in the congregation who had no idea where Patch was going with his demonstration clapped and laughed. I, on the other hand, shaped my face to look as though I was constipated—that was how people in my church looked when disgusted with worldliness, like we hadn't gone to the bathroom for six days.

"Yeah, the kids are really cute, aren't they, moving their little bodies to the soundtrack of hell?" said Patch with a snide grin. "But you see how tempting Satan can be, even leading these precious little babies astray."

By the end of the evening, it seemed that everybody in the music industry either worshiped Satan, was a prostitute, or their brand of hairspray supported a woman's right to choose. Satan was everywhere.

On the following Sunday, my youth pastor, Mr. Billings, sponsored a church bonfire so all of the teenagers moved by Patch's message could once and for all confess their love of Poison, Bon Jovi, or Bette Midler and sacrifice their LPs and cassettes to Jesus. One kid brought his father's entire Beatles collection. Since I wasn't allowed to listen to popular music, I showed up with a mixed tape with one Amy Grant song on it and *The Sound of Music* soundtrack. I surrendered Julie Andrews to the flames for the sake of Jesus.

"I'm proud of you, kids," said Mr. Billings. "You've done the right thing. If you keep making decisions like this one, the devil won't be able to catch you. Just keep fleeing temptation."

Mr. Nelg tossed his algebra book onto his desk, centered himself in front the chalkboard, and fell to his knees. He wiped a tear from his eye and asked us to join him in prayer. Each of us put our faces in our hands. Then Mr. Nelg cried out to God.

"Oh God, hear the voices of your children, crying out for safety and protection from the filth of this land. Save us from the whores and thieves out in Hollywood. We've been trampled by them before, oh God. But God, I don't believe we've ever seen anything like what we're about to see this weekend from the movie *The Last Temptation of Christ*. We pray we never see anything like it again, God. May your soldiers unite! And may we boycott this disgusting, sinful movie! We pray all of this in your holy Son's name. Give us your joy. Give us your love. Amen."

When he opened his eyes, he looked at us very seriously and said, "Our only hope, kids, is that no one will go see *The Last Temptation of Christ*. But until then, I guess I should teach you about the quadratic equation."

Win a Soul,
Win a Prize

Every Thursday night for almost two years, I went door to door in our community and tried to make strangers ask Jesus into their hearts.

It was awkward inviting strangers to confess, especially since we were told to present the gospel in a way that made them think we were doing them a favor. Trying to convince somebody you knew to drop to his knees and repent of his sinful ways was one thing. You were usually aware of a friend's or an acquaintance's sinful ways, and if not, you had enough access to his personal space to research and then make an educated guess. Sometimes you just needed to open a friend's fridge or medicine cabinet to see what he was up to. Find beer or a half-used bottle of vanilla extract? He was an addict. Box of condoms? He was having sex, possibly with strangers. Rolaids or Pepto-Bismol? He felt guilty about his life. With strangers, you didn't have access to any of that information.

"You really do need to repent," I said confidently to

whoever kept their front door open long enough to hear me out. "What if you die tonight? Sure, that might not happen, but one day—could be tomorrow or next Tuesday—you *will* die. Where will you be then?"

I stopped short of telling strangers that I believed this world was little more than a ticking time bomb that could explode into apocalyptic fury at any moment. It scared me, but I spent a lot of time waiting for the end to come.

One Sunday our church invited a prophecy expert to tell us why the end of the world was closer than we thought.

I didn't understand everything he said, but Dr. Gerald Carson didn't seem to offer too much information I didn't already know. I already assumed God was sending earthquakes and AIDS to punish California, and I had heard someone else suggest that the mark of the beast would be a bar code, like the ones grocery stores used to scan products. But I had no idea that a bunch of European nations were having lengthy conversations about becoming one union.

At the end of his talk, Dr. Carson showed us his End Times slide show, which included pictures of catastrophes all over the world, small children who were crying, hungry, and mostly African, and many slides of dark-skinned people wearing turbans. I was afraid.

My youth pastor, Mr. Billings, IBBC's resident expert on the satanic pitfalls of rock'n'roll, believed worrying about the end of the world was a good thing. He encouraged it.

"You should worry!" he shouted during teen church. "Worry for all the lost souls that will die and go to hell because you didn't tell them about Jesus."

I should have worried for that reason, but my anxiety was fueled by a different motivation. My biggest fear about the end was that Jesus would come back before I had the chance to have sex.

I wasn't alone. A lot of teenagers at my church worried about this.

"If Jesus could wait until 1993, I'll have plenty of time to go to college and find a wife," said my friend Roy. "Don't get me wrong—I'm excited about going to heaven, but I've got a couple of earthly needs, if you know what I mean."

I knew what he meant. And listening to him made me worry more, since he was three years older than me and better looking.

"No, man," I said, adding up the years in my head I thought I would need to secure a spouse. "He can't come back until at least 1998! I might need that long."

"Hey, that's cool with me. That will give me a chance to have lots of sex with my wife."

By the end of that conversation, both our virginities hanging in the balance, we made a pact to pray every day that Jesus would wait to return until at least 1998. One of the eighth graders tried convincing us to change our request to 1999, but we told him no.

Mr. Billings thought our concern was ridiculous. My youth pastor was a soul-winning expert, which was why the church hired him. He was responsible for overseeing the youth's preparation for battling against the devil. Pastor Nolan told us that a soul winner was the equivalent to a spiritual warrior, somebody out on the front lines, helping the angels war against the principalities of Satan.

It was hard not to admire Mr. Billings for his spiritual accomplishments. Some estimates suggested more than one thousand souls were going to heaven because of his amazing soul-winning work.

By that time, I'd known Pastor Luke Billings for a number of years. This was his second time working for our church. The first time, he moved to Kent County to be an assistant pastor. The poor guy had hardly settled in to his apartment before the gossip mill was abuzz with rumors. Not about him but about Belinda, his wife.

"Have you seen her, Carole?" asked Leanne, one of my mother's best friends and by far the most informed woman at our church. As she talked, I saw her scratching her right hand with her left. Scratching was always a good sign. Whenever Leanne showed symptoms of hives on her right hand, my mother knew there was something juicy going around about somebody at our church. The more Leanne itched, the juicier the gossip. And since I'd witnessed Leanne apply three applications of hydrocortisone cream during the service, I expected Watergate.

"Seen who?" my mother asked, resting back against a church pew and folding her arms.

"Belinda Billings," Leanne whispered in my mother's ear

and raked the palm of her hand with her fingernails. "The new pastor's wife."

"I haven't seen her. Why do you ask?"

"Let me tell you something." Leanne whispered. "She's a weird one, Carole. *Lunatic* weird. Listen to this. Not only does she apply her makeup thick enough to have gotten an invitation to the native side of the table for the first Thanksgiving"—Leanne looked around to make sure no one was listening—"but the rumor is that her husband has never seen her without it." Leanne nodded, reassuring. "Can you believe that? She gets up at four o'clock in the morning, takes a shower, and puts on her makeup so he doesn't see her."

"Oh, Leanne, you're kidding!" said Mom.

"I wish I was. It gets better, Carole. I hear Luke has never seen her naked, and they've been married for two years."

When my mother finally did meet Mrs. Billings, she put her six months as an LPN at the local mental hospital to good use and diagnosed Belinda as bipolar. "You mark my word, Virgil," she told my father, "that woman is as crazy as a bedbug. A *loon*. We have patients at my hospital who act just like her."

My father didn't take Mom's opinion seriously until the day he and I were driving home from town and saw Belinda hitchhiking in an ankle-length, plaid wool skirt, a black velvet jacket, and dark knee-high boots. She looked as uncomfortable as Diane Keaton in a neck-revealing blouse. Dad immediately pulled over to the side of the road.

"Belinda!" my father yelled. I rolled down the window. When Belinda stuck her face in the passenger's side of the truck, her colorful presence startled me. It looked like something from *Pee-wee's Playhouse* had leaped into our vehicle. I knew it was impolite to stare, but it was difficult to keep my eyes from fixating on her mouth. She'd painted it such a bright shade of pinkish red that her lips appeared to be blinking at me like a broken neon sign. Her blue eyes dazzled, aflame in hues of orange, blue, and purple. She looked like something Picasso painted when he wasn't depressed.

"Do you need a ride?" my father asked.

"Oh no, Virgil," she said. "I'm fine."

"Where are you going?"

"Oh, um." Belinda hesitated. "Actually, I'm on my way to see your wife. I hear she's not feeling well."

"You're going to walk seven miles dressed like that?" my father asked.

"I really enjoy walking, Virgil," she said, running her long fingernails through a few strands of her hair. "It's good for me. I need the exercise."

"It's ninety-five degrees outside."

"I like the hot weather. I'll be okay."

"Come on. Get in the truck."

"Don't worry about me, Virgil. I'm just singing hymns and saying a few prayers."

Dad wouldn't take no for an answer. Eventually, I scooted over, and Mrs. Billings rode home with us.

My mother was right, and a few years later, after the Billingses left Kent County, Belinda sought treatment at a psychiatric clinic in New York. Not long after that, she filed for divorce, and Mr. Billings moved back to work at our church. Normally, the rules didn't allow a divorced man to be a pastor, but a special exception was made since a doctor had ruled Belinda crazy.

I was only fourteen when, one Thursday night, Mr. Billings took a bus full of teenagers into a large housing development and split us up into seven teams of three. The goal was simple: win as many souls for Jesus as we could in ninety minutes. The team that came back to the bus with the highest number of conversions would win a prize.

My friends Katie and Willie were on my team. The three of us had known each other since first grade and were considered the cream of the crop at our church. Each of us had paid our dues with Sunday school attendance and children's choir participation, and our parents had done excellent jobs limiting our interactions with the outside world. Because puberty hadn't kicked in for me yet, I was the holiest of the three. I tried to carry that moniker with pride, but most days I would have traded it for a few strands of armpit hair.

"You should consider that a blessing, Matthew," a teacher said after he heard a classmate tease me for singing higher than the girls. "Nothing undermines a young man's faithful behavior like testosterone."

That confused me. Apparently Jesus was powerful enough to overcome death, but he was no match for the onset of pubic hair.

Our first house was a small white bungalow with a wild, uncut lawn. "Either they're on vacation or this place belongs to a sinner," said Willie, cautiously opening the gate of the chain-link fence. Katie and I followed him up the stone walkway. As soon as Willie rang the doorbell, we heard what sounded like an elephant tap dancing on a hardwood floor. Whoever or whatever was coming to answer the front door had a regular feeding time, and we'd interrupted it.

When the door opened, the largest man I had ever seen towered over us. He wore an Oak Ridge Boys T-shirt and red sweatpants. My eyes were level with the part of his belly that hung out below his shirt. For the first and only time, I wished I were a Girl Scout carrying cases of Thin Mints. Those tasty cookies would have given me a head start if he wanted to eat me.

"Sir," said Willie nervously, "we're from the Baptist church, and—"

"I'm not interested." The man slammed the door in our faces.

When we knocked on the next door, we quickly learned the Jehovah's Witnesses had beaten us to that home's four souls.

"Do you ever get the feeling we're losing the battle?" asked Katie, walking toward the next house. Neither Willie nor I knew what to say.

As we approached the door of a brick ranch house, I noticed a small statue of the Virgin Mary on the front lawn and thought, *Ugh, Catholics.*

I hated trying to win the souls of Catholics for Jesus, because they were convinced they already knew him. "When you witness to Catholics, tell them worshiping Mary is a sin," Mr. Billings had explained. "And tell them God said statues are evil too."

Pastor Nolan said Catholics were going to hell because they followed the pope, and he was convinced the pope would end up being the Antichrist. It had something to do with the word *cat* being in the word *Catholic*.

It was my turn to talk, so when I knocked on the screen door, I took a deep breath. *God, help me.* The door opened, and a black woman, maybe fifty years old and with the most beautiful smile, greeted us.

"Hello, children," she said, swinging the screen door wide open. Her voice sounded rich and deep, almost soothing.

"My name is Matthew," I said. "And this is Willie and Katie. We're from the Baptist church."

"I'm Edie Johnson. Nice to meet you. I've got a friend who is Baptist. She goes to the tiniest church down in North Carolina. I call her my Southern Baptist sweetie."

"Well," I said, "We're *fundamental* Baptist. I don't know the difference between being Southern and fundamental, but it's cool that she's Baptist, I suppose."

"We're all the same in God's eyes, child," she said. "Differences aren't so important as far as I'm concerned."

I smiled, but I sighed on the inside. It was going to be harder than I thought. Not only was this woman Catholic, she was also new age. She probably had a Jane Fonda yoga video next to her VCR.

Pastor Nolan told us Catholicism could be blended with anything. "He's right, you know," a friend's mother had commented. "I visited Haiti in the sixties, and those Haitians went to Mass on Sunday morning, but do you know what they did on Monday? *Voodoo.* Walked around town *practicing* their voodoo. They carried around little dolls, stick pins, and everything. It was scary."

I looked at the string of pearls hanging around Mrs. Johnson's neck and wondered if they were made in New Orleans.

"So, tell me—what brings you kids to my door?" she asked.

"Ma'am, we're out telling people about Jesus," I said. "We don't want anybody to burn in hell, so we're encouraging people to invite Jesus into their hearts."

Mrs. Johnson invited us inside her home. She held the door as we paraded into her green-carpeted living room. A small candle burned on her fireplace mantle, and the faint scent of cinnamon cleared my sinuses. I sat on her velvety couch. By the looks of it, it had been re-covered a time or two, the last as an attempt to brighten up the room. Other than the metallic crucifix hanging on the wall, the pineapple-and-banana-print couch was the shiniest thing in the room.

"So, you children are taking Jesus door to door," said Mrs. Johnson, leaning slowly back against a cushioned rocking chair. "That's very interesting." She put one of her soft brown hands against her chin and leaned her elbow against the arm of the rocker. "I bet you I've invited Jesus to be part of my life several thousand times. In fact, on certain days, I probably ask him two or three times."

"What's the assurance in that?" I asked. "What good is salvation if you have to keep asking for it?"

Mrs. Johnson thought about my question for a moment, taking her time to soak it up. Willie, Katie, and I watched her think. She was interesting to gaze at, a presence that swallowed you up with warmth and mystery.

"Well, Matthew, I don't think there's a formula for getting to know God," said Mrs. Johnson. "I knew a lady about twenty-five years ago. She thought she knew everything there was to know about God. She had him *all* figured out. She'd prance into the cafeteria at work almost every day and tell me what her God thought about my life. 'You shouldn't be doing things this way, Ms. Edie,' she'd say to me. 'God would bless your life if you'd do things this particular way.' One day, when I'd heard all that I could stand, I looked at her and said, 'Ruthie, you might very well have God all figured out in your head, but you're far too judgmental to have him figured out in your heart.' Being a Christian is about constantly learning how to figure Jesus out in your heart, and not just your head.

"That's why I ask Jesus to be part of my life, because I'm a wretched old woman when he's not."

"Mrs. Johnson, do you think you'll go to heaven when you die?" I asked.

"I hope so, Matthew. I'm counting on being there."

"But doesn't it scare you to not know for sure?"

"Scare me?" she chuckled. "Not in the least, child. Besides, how can anybody—except those who have already died—*really,* beyond a shadow of doubt, know for sure? They can't. Nobody can. They can scream as loud as they want to, but that don't change the truth. You see, Matthew, I don't believe God gives us fear. God gives us hope. I am his child. Now, if I'm his child, why would he want me being fearful and scared all the time? That would be like a baby being frightened by her daddy. Think about how you would feel if you were scared of your father all the time. That wouldn't be comforting, now would it?"

"I guess not," I said.

"God loves you, children. He loves you more than you will ever know. Believe that, and you will grow up to do beautiful things."

Mrs. Johnson didn't ask Jesus into her heart, so we lost the contest. One of the other teams went to a house with four kids and a baby-sitter. All five of them asked Jesus into their hearts, and each member of the team won a packet of sea monkeys. You haven't truly witnessed about Jesus until you've done it in hopes of winning a packet of sea monkeys.

I didn't care that we had lost. Not being afraid on the bus ride back to the church was the best prize anyone could have given me.

Piano Boy

By the time I was in tenth grade, Independent Baptist Bible Church had become one of the largest churches on Maryland's Eastern Shore. Each week more than eight hundred people came to our church. One Sunday, our church broke the one thousand mark, and since every member of the church had worked very hard at coercing friends, guilt-tripping co-workers, and picking up hitchhikers in order to reach that goal, Pastor Nolan declared, "No school for Christians!" on the following day. Of course, that was only true for those of us who went to the Christian school.

My church counted lots of things: people, souls, money. We even counted the seconds it took for kids to perfectly quote all fourteen verses of Psalm 19. These numbers were important. High attendance meant the community liked us. Large numbers of souls being saved meant God liked us. Big offerings meant Pastor Nolan liked us. Being the kid with the speediest time in the memory-verse contest just meant free gummy worms.

I did my own counting sometimes.

While sitting through Pastor Nolan's sermons, I often passed the time by counting how many of his "message points" began with the letter *P.* My pastor was prolific with the letter *P.* It didn't matter what topic he spoke on, the *P* words just poured out of him. One Sunday, as he pounded his pulpit, Pastor Nolan powerfully presented potent points about the passion of people who pray, profess, and praise God despite the pain and pestilence of their personal paths.

My pastor picked a peck of *P* words.

But eventually his messages became predictable, and I became bored with them. I'd been sitting through his sermons for eleven years, and I was convinced I'd heard every one of them ten times. They'd become like really loud nursery rhymes. He didn't talk about boys who leaped over candlesticks or felines that played fiddles, but once a month, he said, "I don't smoke and I don't chew, and I don't run with the girls who do." That was usually right after he had yelled and screamed about how awesome it was to live in America and that whoever didn't agree should move to Cuba.

Pastor Nolan's sermons were cruel and unusual punishment for people who had imaginations, sensitive eardrums, or someplace better to be. Since I had long run out of ways to entertain myself, I would have enjoyed hearing about a cat that could play the violin.

One Sunday, I reached a new low and began pretending the end of my finger was a laser beam. While Pastor Nolan preached, I sat in my pew and waited for him to stand under the perfect spot. Then I used my laser to slice through the gold chandelier that hung directly above him and imagined it crashing down on top of him. I didn't want to hurt him—I wasn't violent—I just wanted the church service canceled.

But I feared that, even if I could make the chandelier drop on top of Pastor Nolan, he'd get up and continue preaching just to spite the devil.

So when Clyde Gringleman, a longtime member of our church who went to Bible college so he could be an assistant pastor, offered me the opportunity to volunteer for children's church, I was interested.

Like most of my church's teenagers, I would have done almost anything to get out of sitting through another adult church service. That was why people volunteered to do things during the church hour. The ushers, for example, pretended to be doing official church business so they could get out of listening to the sermon. They stood in the church's vestibule with their arms crossed, and once in a while, one of them would look at his watch and then looked around, as though waiting for somebody to run up to them screaming, "I need God! Quick, can you help me?"

But as boring as that job seemed, I envied every one of those ushers. I would have loved the freedom to stand in the vestibule and pretend to be God's EMT.

"*Please,*" I said to my parents, "can I help Mr. Gringleman? I really want to do this."

Mom and Dad just stared at me, so I continued to plead my case.

"It's not like I'd miss something. Pastor Nolan preaches the same thing over and over again. I mean, how many times do I have to hear that the visitors who come to our church are going to hell?"

My parents looked at each other and then looked at me and then back at each other.

"I'll still go to church on Sunday night and Wednesday night, so I'll only miss one service. Just *one.*"

"You don't even like Mr. Gringleman all that much, do you?" my mother commented.

"I don't *hate* him," I said.

And I didn't hate him. I only thought Mr. Gringleman was odd. I did occasionally wonder whether or not he belonged in a mental institution, but that was because the man ate live goldfish, crickets, and earthworms whenever twenty kids got saved on a Sunday morning, and his way of encouraging us to bring friends to church was telling us he'd jump off the Chester River Bridge if we got fifty visitors to come to children's church. It wouldn't have been suicide, but it would have certainly made the front page of the local newspaper.

I also thought he was pushy with his faith, especially when he tried to evangelize any warm unchristian body able to walk, crawl, wheel, or be carried on a stretcher through the church's front door. Pastor Nolan ordered Mr. Gringleman around like a Labrador retriever: "See that young man wearing the blue shirt and the white-washed dungarees? Go fetch his soul for Jesus!"

Mr. Gringleman would have made a very obedient dog. As soon as Pastor Nolan gave him "retrieving" orders, he ran up the aisle, barked a couple times when he had arrived at the pew, and then dragged the man up the aisle to our church's altar. Then he talked to the visitor for however long it took to get a confession.

Some people called him our church's Columbo, somebody just crazy enough to get anybody in the world to admit they needed Jesus. Mr. G was also the go-to guy whenever the church learned of a non-Christian lying on his or her deathbed. He was the spiritual equivalent to a medevac unit. Even if the one needing Jesus was on life support, in a coma, or lying around in a coffin, it was never too late to try to save a soul's life.

As odd as he was at times, I couldn't *dislike* a man who spent his free time praying with nursing-home residents and sitting with sick people in the hospital.

My parents agreed to let me volunteer but only after I swore it wouldn't affect my Bible quiz competitions. Being on my school's Bible quiz team didn't make me as cool as those on debate team or soccer team or cheerleading squad, but it got me out of the house once a month.

Mr. Gringleman had specifically requested, as he called it, my *musical* expertise. Nobody had ever called me a musical expert before, probably because I wasn't one. I figured Mr. Gringleman had heard that I'd taken almost six years of off-and-on piano lessons and that, with a little intervention from the Holy Spirit, I could likely fake my way through a few children's songs about God. Lucky for the Spirit of God, I could play seven and a half songs perfectly, give or take three. And as it turned out, all the ones I could play really well were songs Mr. Gringleman enjoyed singing.

On my first Sunday as an official volunteer, I felt grown-up being able to tell my friends in Sunday school, "No, I won't be going to church this morning. *Why?* Oh, how should I put this? God ordained me to play the piano for children's church."

The word *ordained* made anything church-related seem more important, almost necessary, as if it were a decision that required me to unlace my high tops in the presence of Jehovah God.

But the only friend who acted like she cared was Fran, which was good, since she was the only person I wanted to care. Fran played the piano better than I did, something she enjoyed throwing in my face, but now I had the upper hand.

"Mr. Gringleman asked *you* to play the piano for junior church?" Fran yelled.

"Yep."

"That's totally unfair. I'm so much better than you."

"I know," I said, warming up my fingers by practicing scales on the air piano in front of me. "That's what makes telling you so much fun."

"I've taken ten years of lessons, Matthew."

"*I know!*" I gleefully ran my fingers across all eighty-eight air keys. "It's almost like there's a conspiracy against you or something."

"You make me sick, Matthew Turner," she said. "Just *sick*!"

"It sounds like you need more church than I do. But listen, maybe I'll recommend you to fill in for me when I'm on vacation."

I wasn't nearly as sure of myself once I sat at the piano bench, waiting for Mr. Gringleman to announce, "Let's sing 'I'm in the Lord's Army'!" I was nervous, but I managed to bang my way through four songs and only needed to stop once to ask Mr. Gringleman if we could start over. He happily agreed. When I finished playing, I walked to the back of the room, leaned against one of the walls, and stood there with my arms crossed and a serious look on my face, waiting for somebody to run up to me with an emergency need for God.

Skipping church felt good.

That Sunday morning, the kid's service had about a hundred and fifty children in attendance. I only knew thirty of them. Most of the kids came to church through the bus ministry. The church owned and operated a fleet of old school buses, painted bronze with the church's name printed across both sides in black. The fleet brought children and teenagers to church. The buses traveled to every part of Maryland's Upper Eastern Shore and even some parts of Delaware to pick up kids. The bus workers spent all day Saturday visiting the homes of those on their bus route to make sure they were coming to church on Sunday morning. I saw thousands of kids and teenagers come through the doors of our church because of the bus ministry. And many of those kids prayed the prayer of salvation.

I listened as Mr. Gringleman stood and asked if there were any first-time visitors in the room. Fifteen children raised their hands.

"If you're a first-time visitor, stand up," he shouted. "Come on, kids! All first-time visitors stand up! We are so glad you joined us this morning, kids! We hope you know that God loves you and we love you too." His voice got serious. "We have some very special information just for first-time visitors we would like to share with you, so please follow Brother Tim out the back door. He's gonna give you some really good information. He'll take good care of you, I promise."

Brother Tim smiled and waved like a car salesman. The fifteen children lined up and followed him out the door.

"Where are they going?" I asked another volunteer who stood close by.

"Oh, just in the room across the hall," he said. "They do this every week."

"What's the special information?"

"The plan of salvation. It's amazing, Matthew. Do you know how many kids have asked Jesus into their hearts since we started doing this?"

I just looked at him.

"Hundreds!" he said. "Our percentages have skyrocketed."

"Percentages?"

"Yeah, the percentage of first-time visitors who get saved each week. I bet nearly every kid in that group comes out of that room born again. I'm serious."

"Really?"

"Yes *sir*. Brother Tim is amazing at leading kids to Jesus. I've never seen anything like it."

"That makes two of us."

"Heaven's got to be jumping up and down, man!"

"Yeah. I bet."

At the end of service, as I walked out of the classroom, I heard two men talking in the hallway. The older one said thirteen out of the fifteen visitors had gotten saved that day.

"Praise the Lord!" the other man commented.

"You can say that again," said the older one. "After last week, we needed some good numbers."

"Were we low last week?"

"Yeah, only two."

"Well, thirteen should help."

"As long we get a decent number of visitors next week, I think we'll be all right."

As I walked toward the front door, I counted my steps, a habit I fell into when trying not to overthink something.

When something bothered me, I had a hard time getting it out of my head. Counting helped me focus, and sometimes it kept me distracted. *Keep counting, Matthew,* I said to myself as I walked toward the church auditorium.

Pastor Nolan had just finished his sermon and was conducting his weekly invitation.

"Every head bowed and every eye closed," said Pastor Nolan. "Nobody looking around."

I stood at the back of the auditorium with my eyes open, looking around the room.

"Somebody might be here right now," he said, "who would say, 'Preacher, I don't know Jesus as my Savior. But I want to know him, so would you pray for me?' If that's you, would you do me a favor and raise your hand so I can pray for you?"

As Pastor Nolan scanned the room, looking for a raised hand, I looked too.

"I see that hand," he said.

I didn't see any hand.

"God bless you," he said. "I see *that* hand."

I looked all around the room, and I didn't see a hand. Pastor Nolan counted five hands.

I counted zero. Maybe I missed them, but I don't think I did. I don't believe anyone raised his or her hand that morning. In time, I noticed that he counted a lot of hands I didn't see.

As the service was about to end, Pastor Nolan smiled and

said, "I've got some good news. Over in the junior church, it seems thirteen children asked Jesus into their hearts and are now on their way to heaven. Let's shout an amen for that."

And then, right before he walked off the stage and invited one of the deacons to close the service in prayer, he shook his head in amazement.

"Thirteen souls. Wow. God is really blessing us."

Benediction

Fundamentalism has little to do with Jesus. It was easy to think it did when I was in the middle of it. I did a lot of talking about Jesus, arguing about Jesus, and contemplating the chances that I could have been Jesus.

Every year, Pastor Nolan handed out an award to the graduating senior he deemed the most like Jesus. It was always given to the student who read their Bible, obeyed the school rules, and had the best publicity. Because the Most Christlike Award was the most heralded award any student could receive, PR was everything.

On the evening I graduated, I looked at Kelley and sighed, "I look stupid, don't I?"

Kelley knew my question was serious, but she didn't know it was also rhetorical.

"*Not* stupid," she said. "You don't look *stupid*. I would tell you if you looked *stupid*. The cap is just a little big, that's all.

But don't worry about it, Matthew. Nobody looks good in a cap and gown."

"What is that supposed to mean?"

That, too, was a rhetorical question, because I knew exactly what it meant. Although I was seventeen and graduating from high school, I looked thirteen. My body was lost somewhere in the belly of the cap and gown, and I looked as though I should have been entering high school, not leaving.

"Mom tells me you're the salutatorian." Kelley adjusted my cap, hoping to find a spot on my head that would make me appear a little older and perhaps human. "Are you excited?"

"A little."

I was excited. I kept it under wraps, but on the inside, I felt happier than the people who jumped up and down next to brand-new Toyotas in commercials. Most students have every right to be excited about being the salutatorian of their class, but most salutatorians have more than four people in their graduating classes. My parents were proud of me, but that was because they didn't know that the bottom two students still didn't know all of their multiplication tables.

"That's the best I can do," said Kelley, referring to her decision to push the cap forward over my forehead, which made the most sense if I wanted my ears to look like flags flying at half-staff on either side of my head. "But still, you don't look stupid."

Our graduation ceremonies were held in the church auditorium, so all four of us met in the church's vestibule. Since my last name began with *T,* I walked in last. Once the four of us were sitting on the front pew, Pastor Nolan stood at his pulpit and said a prayer.

I thought about the words my mother had said to me right before the ceremony began. "You know I'm proud of you, right? I really am."

"Aw, Mom," I said, "I know that."

"I just wanted to make sure."

"We made it through together, huh?" I said.

"Yeah, we did."

After the choir sang, Pastor Nolan announced that year's recipient of the Most Christlike Award, and the room erupted as I walked up to receive my plaque.

I should have been really scared, but I wasn't. I was proud. I was confident.

I was the most like Jesus.

I'm afraid that if I sat down and counted how many church services I've attended, I'd become depressed. It *feels* like I've spent years of my life in church, but it's probably just been a few weeks. When you're trying to impress or influence somebody, though, telling them how you *feel* is almost always better than stating the real facts. Most Christians learn that firsthand while sitting in church. Especially those on praise-and-worship teams.

Since college, I've bounced from church to church, trying to fit into whatever shape my Church of the Moment considered "good Christianity."

I dabbled in Calvinism for a while. Considering myself one of God's exclusives was fun. Like wearing a label: Handpicked by the Almighty to Be One of the Few Who Gets to Be with Him Forever. I had no problem believing that God had chosen me for heaven, but his handpicking others for hell made me weep like a baby. When I left that church, I told a friend, "Well, I suppose I wasn't predestined before the foundations of the earth to be Presbyterian, but I think you might have been."

I've been a member of several nondenominational churches. Most of these churches preached "freedom in Christ," but theirs was freedom that eventually introduced me to a new form of religiosity—a kind that required superhuman strength, guitar skills, and lots of hair gel.

God had a great 401(k) program at those churches. One of the pastors said that God's return on investment was usually ten times the amount he tithed. I started referring to his theology as the Proprietor's Gospel. That church was the only place I knew where the poor in spirit received BMWs, lavish vacations, and their own miniature kingdoms in gated communities. The people at those churches were nice, even compassionate, but most of them lived by a system just as damning as what I lived under as a kid. I always wondered what would happen if they knew the *real* me—the weak and vulnerable me.

I went to a Pentecostal church once. Once was enough.

For about three weeks I considered converting to Catholicism, but I couldn't get into the "sit, stand, kneel, cross yourself" routine. I kept feeling the need to blurt out, *Cross down, when Sally was two,* and clap palms with the man sitting next to me.

I found the most hope—a Jesus kind of hope—at a small country church in Maryland. It had a tight-knit community of a hundred or so believers who really loved one another. Even before I officially joined the church, I experienced love like I'd never felt before. The pastor wasn't the most dynamic preacher, not according to fundamentalism standards, but every time he spoke about the good news, he cried. He felt something. He couldn't always communicate the hope effectively, but he felt it. I had moments when I felt it too.

"Jesus loves you so much." He pulled a white hanky out of his pocket and wiped tears from his eyes as he spoke. "Don't ever let anybody tell you otherwise. No matter what you've done or what you do tomorrow, the Jesus I know *loves* you."

I became involved in that church. I taught Sunday school, helped with the youth program, and sang in the praise-and-worship band once in a while.

And for the first time, I worshiped God without feeling afraid.

My wife and I started going to a new church last year. Cross Point Community meets in the recycled auditorium of an old Baptist church and sits on one of the poorer streets in

Nashville. It's not a perfect church, but I've grown up some and realized there's no such thing as a perfect church.

My church's praise-and-worship music annoys me sometimes. Actually, it's not so much the music I dislike but the light show.

God. Help. The light show.

Some Sundays it's like the aurora borealis on steroids and a timer.

But I've stopped focusing on the light show and recognized it's not hurting anybody. It's not electing presidents, boycotting theme parks, or organizing an apocalypse. It's gaudy beyond repair, but it's harmless.

Besides, many people at my church love the praise-and-worship time just the way it is. Jason, for instance. He's a forty-something recovering alcoholic with perfectly plucked eyebrows and a Botoxed forehead. I don't know him personally, but I see him every Sunday morning. He always sits in the second or third row, denim jacket on, singing and waving his hands toward the heavens. He's one of the happiest guys I've ever seen. I'm not certain, but I think the lights help Jason connect with God in a way.

So I close my eyes during the praise-and-worship time. I try to focus on God and not the multicolored joygasm happening on stage.

That works if I remember to take my Adderall.

Prior to calling Cross Point Community *my* church, I had one very specific need: I wanted the pastor to know my first name. *By heart.* Without having to tell him what letter it started with or that it was one of the books in the Bible. Having the pastor actually *know* Jessica and me seemed important. At our previous church, I got the impression the pastor suffered from short-term memory loss.

Every time we saw him at the mall, the grocery store, or on Sunday mornings in the hug-the-pastor line, it was like we were meeting him again for the very first time. Upon seeing him, my wife and I played three games of Rock-Paper-Scissors. The winner looked at the other and said, "Ha! It's your turn to tell him we've been members of his church for three years."

Every encounter with Pastor Lloyd began with, "Now I know I've seen you somewhere before. Can you remind me of your last name?"

"Turner," one of us said.

"Turner," he echoed. "That's right. I thought it started with a *T.* So good to see you again."

After sharing a big sideways hug, we'd be on our way.

We wanted to avoid the perpetual introduction at Cross Point, so after our second visit I sent Pete, the pastor, an e-mail and asked if we could get together for coffee. By the time our schedules aligned three or four weeks later, I had decided Cross Point was *not* for me. I almost canceled, but for some reason—in perhaps one of those rare moments when God intervenes—I didn't.

We met at Starbucks. I arrived a few minutes before Pete,

and as soon as I sat at one of the outside tables, I started getting nervous.

"I'm so sorry I'm late, man." Pete dropped his belongings in the seat across from me and shook my hand. "You want something? My treat."

"No, I'm good, thanks."

As Pete walked inside to get coffee, my anxiety gurgled from my upper intestine to my lower.

Even though I'm in my midthirties, I still struggle with being alone with a pastor. Furthermore, and more detrimental to my spiritual health, I also have a hard time trusting pastors. Whenever I find myself in the presence of one of God's official spokespeople, part of me clams up with fear. It didn't matter that Pete and I were the same age or that he looked like Ryan Seacrest. I still felt fear.

I feared turning back into the kid who stumbled over words or stuck his foot in his mouth, never felt good enough or worthy, and always suspected that judgment of biblical proportions lay just around the next corner. I've met a good number of pastors who thought they wielded the power of God the way He-Man wielded the power of Grayskull. I'm convinced that a couple of them, when nobody was looking, held their Bibles in the air and screamed, "I am the power." I'm not sure lightning struck at that point, but it should have.

Pete didn't look like the type of pastor capable of calling down fire from heaven—the guy had highlights in his hair— but I didn't know how "close" to God Pete was. Or thought he was. And that mattered. I didn't want to open up to the kind of pastor who believed that, while I told him my story, God was secretly *and inerrantly* revealing the rest of my story to him. I've had pastors make assumptions about me before. I'd tell them a story or two, and they filled in the blanks with their own theories and conclusions about the condition of my soul.

Before Pete sat down, I thought about the advice a therapist gave me. "You have to *work* at trusting, Matthew. It doesn't happen on its own. It's a process—you have to engage."

Easy for her to say—she was an atheist.

"Ah, *coffee.*" Pete had a southern accent, which meant his voice moseyed out of his mouth like it had all the time in the world. "So, you're a writer?"

"I am."

"What kind of books do you write?"

"Christian."

"Really?"

"Well, Christian*ish.*"

"Good. I like those kinds of books better." He laughed. We talked about our favorite authors, our families, and what each of us dreamed about for the future.

"So, Pete," I said eventually, "may I be frank for a moment?"

"Absolutely."

"You're sure?"

"Man, I wouldn't want it any other way."

It's hard being frank with a stranger. Maybe not as hard as

it is sometimes being frank with a friend, but still hard. I didn't know where to begin. Was I supposed to put my finger down somewhere in the middle of my story and start there? It crossed my mind to just confess the truth—that for me, being in the same room with a large group of Christians was about as exciting as a colonoscopy. But I refrained.

"Pete, I'm not very good at doing church." My eyes darted around the coffeehouse scene. "I don't like it all that much."

I waited for Pete to flinch, but instead he grinned.

"That sounds horrible, I know, but it's true," I said. "Right now…I don't like it."

"Dude, I feel that way sometimes. I think that's normal."

"I'm beginning to feel enough freedom to be okay feeling that way. And it's not that I don't want to be a part of a church. Jessica and I both want some of our spirituality to come from the experiences that happen within a church family. We want to serve people. But I don't fit into the so-called evangelical mold. And I don't want to.

"I am passionate about Jesus. I think his death on the cross is so much bigger than what I've been told in the past. I don't—or perhaps I should say *can't*—believe his resurrection was meant to be downsized into one simple equation. That doesn't seem like grace to me.

"What I'm hoping to find in a church is a place all about joining God in the resurrection story. I want to be a part of the solution, not the problem.

"But Pete, I don't know what I believe about the Bible being infallible. I believe it's inspired. I believe it tells God's story. But infallible? I don't know. So, before my wife and I start liking people at Cross Point, I'm wondering if there's a place for somebody like me at your church. Because let's face it—in most of the churches in this town, there wouldn't be a place for me. They wouldn't let me teach Sunday school. A couple might let me usher. But most of them would pray for me to become just like them."

Pete took a drink and told me a story about his first ministry job. I laughed and then told him about the time a church tried to strip me of my volunteer-youth-worker status because I used the word *masturbation.*

"By the way, Jessica wants to know where you get your hair highlighted."

"What?" Pete looked surprised.

"Your highlights. Who does them? She thinks they look natural."

"I don't have highlights."

"You don't?"

"*No.* It's just going gray."

"Are you serious?"

"Dead serious. What? Do I seem like the type of guy who highlights his hair?"

"Uh, sort of…" I shrugged.

"Sort of?"

"Hey—I had highlights once. *In 1999.*"

"So, back when you still had hair."

"I deserved that."

For the record, he still looks like Ryan Seacrest.

Last Sunday Jessica and I went to church. It was Easter. A couple people got baptized. The guy sitting next to me took two smoke breaks. I closed my eyes during the praise and worship. Pete gave a sermon about hope. We took communion.

I wasn't afraid.

Acknowledgments

Jessica, I knew I found a great joy on the day we met, but I didn't know I had found a treasure. You are my dawn, the most precious part of my journey, my dearest friend, and I love you.

To my family—Dad, Mom, Melanie, Kelley, Elisabeth, and also their families—each one of you has shaped my life and given me reasons to laugh and hope. I love each of you so much, and I hope it was okay that I didn't change your names.

My Schim family, thank you for letting me into your lives with such open arms and acceptance.

Much love and gratitude for my community of friends and mentors—Lisa Baker, Julie Price, Lee and Traci Steffen, Daniel and Staci Eagan, Rebekah Hubbell, Pete and Brandi Wilson, Chris Seah, Todd and Angie Smith, Adam Ellis, Tommy Hall, Dixon Kinser, Jennifer Schuchmann, Jason Boyett, Pastor Paul and Marylou Canady, Michael Bianci at World Vision, Cindy Bowdren, Nicci Hubert, Andrea Christian, Matthew Costner, Stephen Lamb, Wade Schuerman, Julie Johnson, Greg Daniel, and Mike Snider and Chris Blaney at Third Coast Artist Agency.

Shannon Hill, you are not only a talented editor, but during this process, you have become a dear friend. Thank you for pushing me out of my comfort zone and, more importantly, helping me remember the comfort zones of others. This book wouldn't be what it is without your guidance and passion for story. I hope this is just the beginning.

Ken Peterson, I can't believe that one of my favorite people in the world is also my publisher. *How did that happen again?* Your kindness and influence have shaped me in so many ways. Thank you for being a mentor, a friend, and giving me the opportunity to tell stories.

To everyone at WaterBrook Press and Random House, thank you for welcoming me into your family of authors with such enthusiasm. Truly, I am grateful.

And to anyone who reads this book, thank you for lending your time to my stories.

Visit Matthew online at
www.matthewpaulturner.com